Self Abuse

Jonathan Self acts as a Special Adviser to the World Land Trust, an environmental charity.

Self Abuse

Love, Loss and Fatherhood

Jonathan Self

Scribner

First published in Great Britain by John Murray (Publishers) Ltd, 2001
This edition published by Scribner, 2002
An imprint of Simon & Schuster UK Ltd
A Viacom Company

The extract on page 195 is reproduced by kind permission of Enid Blyton Ltd,
a Chorion Group Company, from *Five on Finniston Farm*,
copyright Enid Blyton Ltd.

1 3 5 7 9 10 8 6 4 2

Simon & Schuster UK Ltd
Africa House
64-78 Kingsway
London WC2B 6AH

Simon & Schuster Australia
Sydney

www.simonsays.co.uk

A CIP catalogue record for this book is available from the British Library

ISBN 0-7432-3097-3

Typeset by Servis Filmsetting Ltd, Manchester
Printed and bound in Great Britain by
Cox & Wyman Ltd, Reading, Berkshire

For Nat, Jack and Albert

Contents

Fathers

Have you managed any better with your own children?   3

Get yourself stitched up, I am going to bed   13

A complex escape plan   30

Probably old enough to have a Bombshell   40

Mrs Mac, have you stolen my underwear?   56

Hit him back, and hit him harder   72

There was an appalling scene in the kitchen   81

I have a treat in store for you   89

We watched my father hurrying up and down the
flickering beam of light   99

I travelled as Mrs Self   107

Sons

Absolutely rolling in oof   119

He'll drink neat vodka, or ruddy nothing   131

What is this stuff again?   143

You'll have to go to moose school   153

Tell me about your dog's hysterectomy   170

Untruths, half-truths, bent truths and inventions   178

Calculating the misery factor   184

Sixteen conversations with or about my children   191

A phantom child in the wardrobe, building
  a secret den   217

Either he observes the rules or he doesn't play at all   224

Lingering over the remains   229

I was hoping for a better death than this   240

Fathers

Have you managed any better with your own children?

From the age of three I had only one ambition: not to be like my father. I hated everything about him: his smell; the dried, white gunge that gathered in the corners of his mouth; the wax gently oozing from his ears; the strands of greying hair combed across his balding head; his string vests and his woollen long johns; the way he kissed me, with his cold lips pressed against mine, his scratchy beard sand-papering my face, his arms gripping me like a vice, escape impossible; and his loud, baying, penetrating upper-class Englishman's voice. I loathed his meanness with money, his indifference towards my mother, his insensitivity, his slowness, his cowardice, his unwillingness to undertake domestic tasks, his lack of dexterity, his vagueness, his pomposity, his arrogance and the fact that he had little or no sense of humour. Above all else I was appalled by his gaucheness, his lack of style, his social ineptitude.

These negative feelings towards my father were actively encouraged and almost certainly originally engendered by my mother, who managed with considerable emotional agility to revile and adore him simultaneously. One moment she would be instructing my younger brother Will and me to give him a slow hand-clap when he arrived home from work: 'Here's the old goat, now, show him what you think of him, children.' The next she would be cuddling and hugging him and telling us that 'He is the greatest man alive. Try to grow up to be as wonderful. God, I love your father.'

Love, however, was not a word that ever escaped from my father's lips.

'I am fond of your mother.'

'I am fond of you boys.'

'I am very fond of Brownie.' Brownie was the family dog.

Fond. Was he saying that he didn't actually love me? It was impossible to tell. In my father's world it was not done to discuss or display any real feelings.

'Your mother', he once commented as she silently and systematically applied herself to the task of smashing all the best crystal glasses, 'is slightly upset.'

'Sadly your grandfather has died,' he announced after breakfast one morning.

'It's a dreadful shame,' when informed that his youngest son was addicted to heroin.

Much as it is human nature to stare at a road accident even though we know it is going to upset us, the temptation to ask my father what he meant by the word 'fond' became irresistible.

'It means . . . well, it means that I am fond of you,' he stated.

I pressed him to be more specific. As I spoke tears began to well up in my eyes. 'But, do you love me, Dad?'

He stared at me, as at a stranger. 'I suppose', he answered eventually and as if it were a matter of only transitory interest, 'I must.'

My father was not a man who hurried. His speech, even when agitated, was always measured. He took longer to eat a meal than anyone else I've ever met (though not as long, he proudly insisted, as his grandfather, who 'masticated' a staggering forty times before swallowing each bite). Movement from one place to another, whether a visit to the local shops or a journey overseas, could only be embarked upon after ponderous consideration and detailed planning. At some level I think he believed it to be bad form to rush.

Consequently the trip from London (where I spent most of my childhood) to Brighton (where we had an apartment in my grandparents' house), despite being no more than seventy miles, was, so far as my father was concerned, a six- or seven-hour drive allowing for one meal stop (usually Cowfold for lunch or tea and a stroll around the churchyard in order to inspect the family graves) and one walk (invariably a climb to the top of Box Hill or the Devil's Dyke). Such fathering as I received, and there wasn't much of it, occurred for the greater part while we were in transit. Once my father had me trapped in the car, or unwillingly coerced into joining him on his daily walk, he lost no opportunity to proffer what I suppose he imagined to be invaluable paternal advice. This advice came in several distinct forms. There were oft-repeated generalities: 'Don't over do it, darling'; 'You would be happier if you played a sport. Why don't you take up golf?'

There were warnings: 'Be careful in business: there are a lot of sharks in business'; 'You'll make yourself ill if you work too hard.'

There were insights: 'Women are complex'; 'Money isn't everything.'

And there were health tips: 'Come for a swim in the sea, it will do you good'; 'Why don't you go and stay with Francesca in Walberswick? It would perk you up.'

Staying with people was something at which my father excelled. Knowing no shame, needing no encouragement, oblivious to doubts expressed by even the most unwilling of hosts, he boldly notified the chosen ones by telephone: 'Ah, Bartle, it's Peter . . . I was thinking how nice it would be to see you . . . we can make it for two nights on the twenty-third.'

Bartle, he assures my mother, will be delighted to have us, just as, on a different occasion, he assures her that Christopher will be delighted to have us. Christopher and my father shared a study at boarding school. They haven't stayed in touch but my father knows roughly where he lives.

The family car (a converted Post Office van, painted grey, with extra seats in the back) is parked outside a public call box on a deserted stretch of road somewhere in the Welsh border country. My father is inside the kiosk with a pile of big old copper pennies trying to track down Christopher. My mother has wound the car windows up because she doesn't want to hear my father talking on the telephone but we can anyway, his voice booming at the operator.

'No, no, no. Try spelling it with an M.'

It is six or seven in the evening. We've had no supper. Will has fallen asleep. My parents have been bickering all afternoon as we follow my father around various historic monuments. He is persistently refusing to pay for us to stay in a bed and breakfast.

'In 1642 –' he begins, pointing to some distant hills.

'This was intended to be a holiday,' my mother cuts in. 'What sort of holiday do you call this?'

'You are right, darling. We should have bought a larger tent.'

'*You* should have bought a larger tent. I told you this one didn't have enough room in it.'

Indeed, the new tent had proved so small that on the previous night my father had announced he would have to stay in a hotel in order to make more room for the rest of us. He made it sound as if it were a matter of deep, personal regret that he wouldn't be sleeping in the bosom of his family: that it was a painful sacrifice. While my mother was wrestling with guy ropes he simply strolled away. When she looked up from where she was kneeling, mallet in hand, and he was gone, she began to cry. Will and I tried to comfort her but she kept shrugging us off. Later we fell asleep to the sound of her sobbing.

In the morning my father reappeared while my mother was

cooking sausages over a portable gas stove. My brother and I watched him ambling down the lane towards us. (We were camped on the verge: 'Why waste money on an official site? It is just a swindle.') He was swinging his walking stick, sniffing the air, smoking a cigarette.

'Ah, there you are, Bunchy,' he greeted my mother. Bunchy was what he always called her. I can't remember him ever addressing her by her real name, which was Elaine.

'Don't you fucking there-you-are-Bunchy me,' she began, but he ignored her.

'Had your breakfast yet?'

She retorted through gritted teeth: 'What does it look as if I'm doing?'

But he affected not to notice. Perhaps he genuinely did not. 'No? Well, I'll go back to the hotel and have another cup of coffee and you can pick me up when you're packed.'

He turned on his heel and as he walked away she began to hurl objects into the van: half-cooked sausages, clothes, the hot stove, the greasy frying pan, the tent – everything mixed in together. My brother and I tried to help her; however, this only seemed to anger her more. In the end Will climbed into the back seat clutching his teddy and sat there with his eyes shut, whimpering. I stood awkwardly to the side wishing I were dead.

Once we were on our way my father could no longer avoid her wrath. Yet for each criticism she raised, he came back at her with an objection.

'How can you say I am insensitive?'

'I would remind you that I am the man who –'

'I'm sorry, darling, but you're wrong.'

'If you had told me how you'd felt at the time, of course, I wouldn't have –'

'Don't talk bally rot.'

Will and I didn't really understand what they were fighting

about, but one thing was certain, my father wasn't going to pay for a bed and breakfast.

'There is plenty of time to sort out our accommodation after we have had a pleasant day sightseeing,' he insisted whenever my mother raised the topic.

Perhaps he planned to introduce the idea of staying with the unknown Christopher all the time. Maybe it had only struck him as nightfall approached. Either way he is in the telephone box and we're waiting. Finally he emerges: 'It's OK,' he says, tapping on the window with his knuckle to indicate he wants the door opened for him, 'Christopher will be delighted to have us.'

It takes an age to find Christopher's place and before we arrive I, too, have fallen asleep. Vaguely I recall being lifted out of the car and placed in a strange bed still warm from someone else's body.

When I awake I lie rigid for what seems like hours, my eyes squeezed shut, hoping that my mother will come and rescue me. The sheets are softer than the ones we have at home and smell distinctly of another child. I can hear breakfast being eaten in some distant part of the house, my father's voice rising and falling above the clinking of cutlery and crockery. My mother doesn't come and doesn't come and eventually, desperate for a pee, I slide out of bed and explore. The room I've been sleeping in is tiny – a labyrinth of bunk beds, chests and wardrobes which tower threateningly above me. The hallway also overflows with furniture – mostly bookshelves – and the lavatory door is jammed open with cardboard boxes filled with clothes. I can't get the door closed and so I go quickly, fearing that someone will appear unexpectedly and see me.

Shyly I descend to the kitchen and stand out of view listening. My father's voice is distinct now. He is lecturing whoever is in there on politics.

'I disagree, Buffy, I disagree completely. If you don't mind me saying so you made a similar error of judgement about Chamberlain when we were at Lancing. Harold Wilson is the best chance –'

I have not hidden myself sufficiently well and my father breaks off mid-speech because he has caught sight of me.

'Ah, here's Johnny. He has a better grip on politics than you do, Buffy. Come in, darling, and have some kedgeree.'

There is no escape. Conscious that everyone is watching me – and that everyone consists of a great number of unknown adults and children – I creep to a corner of the huge table and perch half on, half off a rough wooden bench. My mother is at the other end of the table concentrating on feeding Will. She doesn't even glance in my direction. A bowl of kedgeree is placed in front of me. I've never had kedgeree before and the smell of the fish makes me feel nauseous. Only my father speaks.

'Mmm, this kedgeree is delicious,' he declares, smacking his lips in an exaggerated manner, 'you eat it up, Johnny, it will be good for you.'

Later, when we are on our way, he says in a triumphant voice: 'There, I told you that Christopher would be delighted to have us.'

'Couldn't you see,' I long to scream at him, 'couldn't you see that the opposite was true? That he obviously doesn't like you? That he and his wife and his children didn't say a word to any of us while we were in their house? That he has an enormous family and a minute home and that we were imposing on them, stretching a highly tenuous friendship to breaking point? Can't you understand that your wife, your sons, every single person with whom you come into contact finds you repugnant?' But, of course, I cannot voice these thoughts coherently and instead sit miserably in the back seat leaving my mother once again to take up the cudgel.

I'll say this for my father: he was rarely perturbed or upset

9

by personal attacks. If he had read this, for instance, he would have been more concerned with identifying errors of fact: 'It wasn't the Welsh borders, darling'; 'For accuracy's sake, I must point out that your mother was responsible for choosing the tent we purchased.'

In preparing what he would view as a logical defence: 'Remember, I never wanted to marry your mother. She knew I was in love with someone else'; 'Don't forget, your mother was an extremely neurotic and volatile woman.'

And in launching a counter-attack: 'Have you managed any better with your own children?' 'I think you are being very ungrateful. I took you boys to some marvellous places. We weren't rich, you know. I only had a professor's salary and a small private income.'

My father seemed positively to relish even the most savage criticism. I attribute this to the fact that he was the emotional equivalent to being deaf: if what you said wasn't extreme he couldn't hear you. In order to satisfy an instinctive need to feel some emotion – any emotion – I even suspect that he may subconsciously have encouraged attack. Nor should it be forgotten that he was brought up in the public school and Oxford tradition of debating – where winning an argument is more important than which side you're on.

My father loved winning and was a bad loser. If anyone beat him at a game, for instance, he would invariably challenge their victory, refusing to concede no matter how compelling or conclusive the evidence against him. Should he be forced to acknowledge defeat, he would analyse and dissect every stage of the contest, explaining to whoever would listen where he went wrong and in what ways he was poorly treated. In this respect he had an insatiable capacity for self-pity.

For my father, every conversation, no matter how trivial the topic, held out the glorious possibility of a disagreement. In the opening stages of any dialogue he was, therefore, normally careful to remain non-committal in order to ascertain precisely what line the other party intended to take. Once a definitive statement or decision had been elicited, he was then free to take the opposing view.

'What would you like to do this evening, Dad?'

'Oh, I'm adaptable.' Adaptable was a favourite expression.

'Well, would you enjoy eating out?'

'I'm terribly easy. Whatever you want.'

'Anywhere you prefer?'

'As I say, I am completely adaptable. You decide.'

'I'll book Browns.'

'Browns? What? That place? Don't be an ass. It is a frightful clip joint. If that's your idea of an evening's entertainment I'd rather stay in.'

'Fine, I'll cook.'

At this point it was his ardent hope that the discussion would become more heated. If it didn't he would attempt a little light goading.

'I am surprised you're wedded to the idea of Browns. If you don't mind me saying so, you are extremely inflexible in your habits. Not just over restaurants.'

Should this fail to hit the mark he would make a wild and controversial statement, throwing it out casually, yet fully aware of its potency.

'If this is what Jo and Perrie had to suffer, no wonder they both left you.'

In anyone else, switching the subject away from a domestic arrangement to the total breakdown of two marriages in such a short period of time could only be construed as malicious. Not in my father's case, though. What he did was beyond his control; deeply embedded in his psyche. He had absolutely no insight into the way in which he behaved. Were he to have comprehended the profoundly disturbing effect he had on me, I'm sure he would have been appalled.

I used to have a speech on the subject ready and rehearsed:

'Dad, I don't want to offend you, but there is something I need to explain to you. Whatever I say, you seem to contradict me for the sheer pleasure of it. You argue over matters which are unimportant to either of us. You seek out controversy whenever and wherever possible. Furthermore, you speak with devastating conviction regardless of your true beliefs. You are never conciliatory. Nor do you hesitate to deliver emotional body blows or to launch unprovoked attacks. However I respond to you, I feel I lose out. If I ignore your attempts to start a debate, I suffer – holding back my anger as you try different and increasingly hurtful ways to draw me into an argument. If I engage, it soon descends into a bitter row. Worst of all, I have developed a similarly argumentative and dismissive conversational approach myself. My family, friends and work colleagues endure from me precisely what I have been forced to endure from you. I bear the guilt of perpetuating something which I myself abhor. What guilt do you bear?'

It's OK, Dad, I can answer for you.

'I am sorry to hear this, Johnny, very sorry. I had no idea you felt so strongly, dear boy. But, with respect, I cannot completely believe you. Nor can I totally agree with your assessment of –'

The thing about my father was he had to be right.

Get yourself stitched up, I am going to bed

Where my father was slow and cautious, my mother was quick and impetuous. Where he was mean and careful with money, she was generous and a spendthrift. Where he was mild mannered and difficult to anger, she was passionate and irascible. If I describe my father as being one thing, you can be certain that my mother was the opposite.

My father avoided shouting, scenes or any visible display of feeling. He was not physical. He was not affectionate. He rarely, if ever, discussed his innermost thoughts. He was somewhat detached from even his closest family and friends. My mother, on the other hand, was loud. She was emotional. She touched and hugged. She expressed herself freely and volubly. Far from being detached, she did not hesitate to involve herself in other people's lives and affairs. Furthermore, she was dominant, opinionated, and intolerant of anyone who disagreed with her or refused to fall in with her plans.

It is not easy to do full justice to the complex nature of my mother's personality. The only consistent thing about her was her inconsistency. For instance, I could honestly describe her as being both kind and vindictive; open-minded and judgemental; caring and destructive. So if I tell you she was like this, or like that, and then a little later on appear to contradict myself, please do not assume that I am confused or uncertain or exaggerating. It is simply that she had many, often conflicting traits. For this reason you could never quite be certain how you stood with her. One minute you might be in favour, the next in disgrace, without any apparent reason for her change of heart.

'Pssst.'

I looked up. My mother beckoned to me from the kitchen. 'What?' I got up slowly from where I was sitting at the bottom of the stairs, dropped the book I had been reading, and reluctantly moved towards her.

'Ssshhh.' She held a finger up to her lips. The house had only just settled down after a row between my brother and me. Banished from the drawing room because my father was writing, we had gone upstairs to play. A squabble had broken out over ownership of some Lego and my mother had forcibly separated us, ordering me to sit at the bottom of the stairs and read, while Will had been allowed to take possession of the toys in question and to return, unmolested, to our bedroom.

'Listen to me.' My mother spoke in a conspiratorial whisper.

'What?' I replied sulkily. I knew that she was going to ask me to set the table for supper.

'Just do as I say. Go and get your coat on, sneak around the back of the house and wait by the car. Don't get into it until I order you to. Bring your book.'

'Why?'

'Just do as I say. Go.'

Wonderingly, I obeyed. A few minutes later she appeared, also wearing a coat and carrying a book. She bent down and put her mouth to my ear.

'When I say "now" get into the car as quietly as you can but don't slam the door. Just hold it nearly closed. Nod if you understand.'

I nodded.

14

'Now.'

We got in, she released the handbrake and the car ran backwards down the drive. Once we had reached the street she started the engine.

'Slam your door. We've made it. They can't stop us now.' She was exultant.

'Where are we going? What about supper? What about Will and Dad?'

'I doubt that either of them will notice we aren't there before we get back, but if they do they can forage. As for you and me – I thought we would have a hamburger, and a milkshake, and chocolate cake, and ice-cream, and a Reading Supper in a restaurant for a change. Just the two of us, without your stupenagle brother and your wretched father.'

I tingled with excitement. We were alone, together, on a secret adventure. The ten-minute journey to the restaurant seemed daring and unconventional. The atmosphere in the car was intimate.

'Johnny?'

'Yes?'

'I am sorry I took Will's side.'

'That's OK, Mum.'

'I am afraid that I have other things on my mind.'

'What sort of things?'

'Grown-up things.'

'What sort of grown-up things?'

'Mostly to do with your father.'

'Oh.'

'I am afraid that we fight a lot.'

'I fight a lot with Will.'

'Will doesn't do the sort of things to you that your father does to me.'

'He takes my toys.'

'I know, darling, and I said I was sorry.'

15

'I didn't mean it that way, Mum.'

'I feel awful that you hear your father and me fighting. But I am afraid your father doesn't always treat me as well as he should.'

'I understand, Mum. I know it can be bad for you. I know Dad can be horrid.'

Suddenly, a change of mood. She surprised me with her laugh.

'Oedipus, schmoedipus,' she said. It was an expression she used a great deal and though I didn't understand what she meant by it, I laughed, too.

'How is school going? Is that little bastard Gavron still giving you a difficult time?'

He was, and she listened sympathetically as I explained how he had pushed me over during morning break and spat on my blazer. My tale of woe lasted until we reached our destination. When she had found a parking place she took me in her arms. 'Quiet, now. Everything will be all right. Forget Gavron and enjoy your supper.'

I yielded willingly to her embrace.

'You are my favourite,' she said, and I flushed with pleasure, choosing not to hear the rest of the sentence, 'in your age group.'

My mother's life centred on two great passions: food and books. Reading Suppers combined both and were staged once or twice a week. Normally she would prepare a meal which required minimal serving – frankfurters in baked beans or lasagne, for instance – and the three of us (my father was never present on these occasions) would eat in enforced silence at the kitchen table, heads bent over as we read, automatically spooning ourselves extra helpings until all the food was gone. After the main course my mother would produce a homemade cake or cookies and we would sit munching contentedly, drinking glass after glass of milk, each of us totally absorbed in our book. Reading Suppers were always billed as a special event; and, as such, were an excellent example of how my mother used food and the process of eating to make life more enjoyable. At every juncture food was promoted as being the ultimate treat and our lives revolved around what we ate, when, and why we were eating it. It was often used crudely, as in: 'Go upstairs to the bathroom and fetch my glasses and I'll give you a Mars bar for breakfast.' But mostly it was deployed in a more subtle manner to alleviate boredom, to mask unhappiness, and to compensate for pain. Food which my mother probably intended to serve anyway would be utilised to create a sense of excitement and drama: 'Listen, kiddiwinks. We deserve a break, something to cheer us up. I'll make a huge bowl of spaghetti and a mountain of raw carrots and we'll have a party.' As well as to comfort us: 'I know you boys hate me arguing with your father. I'll make you some poached eggs on toast and bacon and you'll feel better.'

Presentation was critical. The best china, the real silver and the crystal glasses would be brought from the dining room for a kitchen meal of lamb chops and frozen peas. A snack of apple and raisins would be put into a brown paper bag and served to us at bedtime: 'Right, boys, first one into bed gets a goody bag –'

The food itself was different because my mother was American. Hamburgers and brownies, meatloaf and pecan pie, hot dogs and sundaes were part of our diet long before they became commonplace in the UK. She particularly liked to entertain, and people were forever dropping in for a little bite of something. Anyone who rang up was liable to receive a spontaneous invitation and many of her telephone conversations were followed by a bellowed announcement: 'Emma Fisher is coming for pancakes and maple syrup'; 'Ruth will be here for dinner'; 'Your aunt Penny is on her way over for coffee and a sandwich.' After which she would charge into the kitchen to get everything ready. Really, my mother was never happier than when preparing nourishment for others.

Except, perhaps, when she was reading. Food may have consoled her, but books were her sanctuary. She read for a minimum of two hours a day. When she was depressed, which was frequently, she read for even longer. It was not unknown for her to spend all day in bed reading. If for some reason she couldn't read, she became grouchy and went about the house complaining. Like many people who turn to books as an escape from the real world, my mother's dependency began as a child. Her mother – Grandma Lily – was petite, delicate and beautiful, and couldn't forgive her daughter for being large, ungainly and unattractive. Grandma Lily did not keep her disappointment to herself, either, but used to taunt my mother: 'You are fat, fat, fat'; 'Couldn't you try to be less clumsy?' 'You are too big, too ugly and too stupid ever to find a husband.'

Later, Grandma Lily was proved wrong on this final point (twice, as it happens), but at the time my mother's response was to creep quietly away to her room and read. This infuriated Grandma Lily, who never so much as opened a book, and she bombarded my mother with dire warnings: 'You are ruining your eyes with all that reading. You'll wear them out. You'll squint and no man will ever look at you.'

Books played a critical role at every juncture of my mother's life: they got her to university; they got her work; and they helped her to attract the men that Grandma Lily had said would never be interested. More than this, they gave her status. This was particularly true when she came to England in the 1950s. She may have been an outsider – American, Jewish, divorced and from a poor background – but she was exceptionally and undeniably well read. Faced with the crushing superiority and deep-rooted (if cleverly disguised) prejudices of the English upper classes, my mother's understanding of literature helped not only to save her from overwhelming feelings of inadequacy and inferiority but also to win friends. Who could fail but to be impressed by her knowledge of fiction, the classics, biography, autobiography, travel, food and history writing? She was a fast learner, too, and with Nancy Mitford's invaluable tome to guide her she soon became the epitome of everything that was 'U'.

To ensure that her bookishness did not go unnoticed, my mother made a great display of her love of the printed word. She carried a canvas book bag with her wherever she went; she haunted little-known libraries; and she carefully arranged piles of seemingly haphazardly stacked books at strategic points around the house. As a consequence of their importance in her life, books became sacred items, to be worshipped and revered. You never disposed of a book; and their acquisition became my mother's main objective in life. The greatest crime in our family was to damage, deface or destroy a book. It was forbidden to turn down the corner of the page to mark your place, and writing in a book (even pencil notes in the margins of a textbook) would automatically bring on one of my mother's rages.

She had a dreadful temper and it took only the slightest of incidents, or the mildest of comments, to unleash the full force of her anger. Her wrath may have been extreme, but it was also shortlived; almost as if a switch had been flicked on and then off. Because there did not have to be a rational explanation for her sudden change in mood, it was difficult to anticipate and all the more frightening.

'Get out.'

My mother didn't look around when I entered the kitchen but continued to work at the counter with her back to me. I stood in the doorway wondering what I had done to irritate her.

'You heard,' she spoke evenly, without emotion, 'get out.'

She was preparing the dog's food – stabbing chunks of sickly smelling meat from the can with a fork, and transferring them to a stainless-steel bowl.

'Why?'

No reply. She tapped the fork repeatedly against the rim of the bowl with unnecessary vigour – clack, clack, clack – in order to dislodge a particularly glutinous chunk of meat and then began to scrape feverishly at the bottom of the can. She was making so much noise that perhaps she hadn't heard me.

'Why?'

'Why? What does it matter? I asked you politely to get out. Go. Leave. Find somewhere else to reside. You are fourteen and reasonably intelligent. You work it out. I don't want you in the house any more.'

Not for one second did I doubt the sincerity of her words. I was overcome by panic. Where could I go? How would I support myself? I blurted out in words that seemed to come from someone else – thin, distant, reedy, high-pitched words – an appeal: 'But, Mum –'

My fear seemed to infuriate her. She turned suddenly to face me, eyes blazing, features contorted with rage.

'Get out. Get out. Get out. Just fuck off like your father did. This is no longer your home.' She was ranting now.

I began to cry. 'Mum, Mum –'

'Don't Mum me, you little prick. I don't care where you go, or how you get there, or what happens to you after you've gone. Just get out. Get out, and take your fucking dog with you.'

She kicked the dog, who yelped and shot past me, whimpering.

'And its fucking food.'

Without warning she snatched up the tin of Chum and flung it in my direction. It caught and cut my wrist before clattering on to the hall floor behind me. Blood from the wound ran in rivulets down the palm of my hand, tracing a speedy progress around splattered lumps of dog food, before splashing from my fingertips on to the linoleum below. My mother said nothing but yanked open a drawer and pulled out some tea towels. She came towards me and instinctively I ducked – only a few months earlier she had broken my arm, by twisting it behind my back when she'd found me snooping in her wardrobe – but she pushed past, shoving the towels at my chest as she went.

'Tie them round your wrist. Then take the Underground to the Whittington Hospital and get yourself stitched up. I am going to bed.'

There is a type of person who can show unfailing love to others, but not always to themselves, or to their immediate family. That's how my mother was. Which is why, at the party we held after she died, more than a hundred people came to mourn and – with the aid of cheap wine, cubes of cheese on cocktail sticks and paper handkerchiefs – weep copiously over their collective loss with an intensity of grief which neither I nor my brothers were able to feel.

'No one was ever so kind or considerate to me as your mother,' wailed a man I had never seen before, tears streaming down his face.

'She was my best friend, my only friend,' sobbed another total stranger.

'A wonderful, giving spirit,' quietly and sadly from someone with a terminal illness whom my mother had visited regularly.

'There is a huge, rotten, Elaine-shaped hole in my life,' bemoaned a neighbour. 'How I shall miss her.'

Who were these people talking about? A large, energetic,

restless sort of a woman who responded instinctively, unhesitatingly, to the needs of anyone, everyone with whom she came into contact – embracing their anguish, disappointments, uncertainty, fear, anger and inability to cope as if they were her own. A woman from whom it was impossible to hide your innermost thoughts and feelings – for not only did she have a disturbing ability to sense when there was something wrong, but she could identify the nature of the difficulty with unnerving accuracy. A woman who was capable of endearing herself to those whose lives she touched by the determination and zeal with which she attempted to solve their problems and ease their suffering.

My mother's constituency was large and disparate. At one end of the spectrum were hundreds, if not thousands, of immigrant Asian women whom she had rescued from domestic isolation by setting up English classes for them in order that they could learn the language which their husbands and children had already mastered in the workplace and at school. At the other end an eclectic mix of close friends: an ageing homosexual peer who had been involved in an infamous public scandal; a brilliant but alcoholic scholar who never managed to complete a single work; a liberal, exiled South African lawyer who was dying of cancer; a publisher whose baby daughter could have been begotten by any one of six possible fathers. The members of my mother's inner circle were fascinating and troubled.

There was an endless, perpetually expanding list of acquaintances, too. So many, in fact, that she had to keep notes against their entries in her address book to remind herself who they all were: 'Jane Waldron. Plane from Pisa. February 1979. Suicidal boyfriend'; 'Philip Rout, Honfleur, homosexual, shingles. Garlic (?)'; 'Lucy ——, queue for Kenwood concert. Interview skills.'

Thus innumerable encounters were recorded, each of

which invariably resulted in my mother taking on a self-appointed task of one kind or another. Jane Waldron would have been recommended to a remarkable therapist specialising in suicidal boyfriends; Philip Rout would have been sent a cure for shingles, perhaps involving garlic (in my mother's eyes garlic was nature's miracle drug and she broached no criticism of its powers); and Lucy (without a surname) probably received a book on how to do better in interviews. My mother's progress through the world was marked by such acts of kindness. She was forever seeking out projects to complete on behalf of others and she had a touching, if somewhat naive belief that she was 'making a difference'. I think she saw herself as being mildly divinical.

This is not to trivialise my mother's genuine concern for others, nor to discount the good she clearly did. But there was something unhealthy about the way she identified with every member of the human race who happened to stray across her path. It was not simply that she spoke to strangers; she spoke to all strangers.

My ex-sister-in-law, Annie, relates a story about travelling with my mother on a bus in Italy.

'Tell that woman she has a beautiful baby,' instructed my mother, who spoke not a word of Italian, but didn't view it as a barrier to communication.

Annie, somewhat reluctantly, complied. Within minutes my mother and the Italian woman were both chivvying Annie to translate faster as they compared medical notes. The woman had recently lost her oldest child and began to cry hysterically. My mother, not to be outdone, began to cry hysterically, as well. For Annie, who abhors any public display of emotion, this must have been as close to hell on earth as it gets. Conversely, for my mother, it must have been an extremely satisfying experience – fulfilling her constant yearning to create meaningful relationships out of the slightest and most

23

insignificant of chance meetings. Women on buses, taxi drivers, waitresses, traffic wardens, people in the street – all had to be charmed, won over, made to feel that they shared a common bond with my mother, a special place in her heart.

She was black and white about people. You were either her friend or her foe. The first stage of acceptance into the former category was to submit to (or better still to participate in) a detailed analysis of what was wrong with your life. To this end it was necessary to extract details of your secrets and your sorrows, a task my mother performed using a methodology that owed more to surgery than psychology. Her anaesthetic was the application of intimate and deeply personal confidences.

'How am I today? Thank you for asking,' I once heard her reply to the casual enquiries of an anonymous bank clerk who could hardly be seen through the security grille, 'but I have made a hash of two marriages, I am over fifty, I am a dress size eighteen, and I feel miserably unhappy. Still, nobody said life would be perfect.'

Her scalpel was the direct question: 'I see you are married. Tell me, do you still love your husband?'

She did not accept rejection of her own candour or questioning of others, and a cool response from someone previously singled out as a potential ally would cause her to become icy and dismissive. As she parted company with the person concerned she would make loud, disparaging comments: 'She wasn't friendly. I wonder what her problem was? I certainly didn't like her.'

But those who opened up, who engaged, were rewarded with my mother's undying loyalty and devotion. Acceptance of a new friend was invariably signalled in the same way. Placing her hand on their arm, and looking them straight in the eyes, she would utter one of her favourite and most used phrases: 'You can come to my birthday party.'

The words were spoken in a girlish tone which managed simultaneously to be both coy and sardonic. There was no birthday party, of course, and the invitation was wholly disingenuous. What my mother was really doing was conferring her blessing on the recipient who, thereafter, was 'in' and could do no wrong.

Because my mother's reaction to people was unpredictable, introducing her to my friends and lovers was fraught with tension. I distinctly remember bringing my girlfriend Perrie home to meet her for the first time. As we arrived outside, my mother's dressing-gowned form appeared rather suddenly and not a little menacingly at a first-floor window. Clearly, she had been lying in wait for us. A tortured screeching sound as she yanked open the casement (the banging and clanging of the lead weights clearly audible in the street) and there she was, her huge face hanging threateningly above us like a demented gargoyle.

'Fuck. Fuck. Fuck.'

The words echoed round and round the sleepy stuccoed crescent as if desperately trying to find some means of escape, before eventually fading away in the direction of Tufnell Park.

'Where the fuck have you been?' she yelled down to us. 'Where? Where? Where?'

'This is Perrie,' I explained.

My mother ignored me. 'You are late and I asked where the fuck you have been. Bob and Ranette have been here for fifteen minutes waiting for you.'

'But you asked me to collect them from my house and as they weren't there we hung on for them.'

'Oh, never fucking mind. The food is fucking ruined.'

My mother withdrew her head. I squeezed Perrie's arm reassuringly and we climbed the steps to the front door. We were buzzed in.

'This is Perrie.'

My uncle Bob struggled up from the sofa to shake hands. Aunt Ranette trilled a 'hello' from the kitchen area.

My mother could be heard slamming things in the bedroom. I tried to catch Perrie's eye; she had turned quite pale. Bob chatted with her on the sofa and I helped my aunt with lunch.

After an age my mother emerged, fully dressed, and perfectly composed. She showed not the least sign of embarrassment.

'Hello, have a glass of wine,' she said to Perrie, as if nothing untoward had occurred. And by our family's standards, of course, nothing had. My mother had simply had a tantrum because things had not gone as planned.

It was this same unfortunate compulsion to control even the most inconsequential events which continually led her to make rash decisions and ill-considered judgements. Relationships were ended, opportunities lost, money wasted, hardships endured all because my mother couldn't allow anyone else to influence even the smallest part of her life. It didn't matter to her that she might suffer unnecessarily, if it meant that she governed the outcome of any given situation. Naturally, she attempted to exercise absolute control over her children. The success with which she managed to impose her authority is illustrated by the first words which came to me when I began to write about her: 'I am possessed by the spirit of my mother. She is inside me: the ghost in my works. My thoughts, my mood, my actions, are all – to a greater or lesser extent – predicated by someone who has been dead for over ten years. Feverishly from beyond the grave she manipulates me, dominates me, determines my destiny.'

My mother had, to use one of her own expressions, a 'whim of iron'. Her rule was absolute and she enforced it through a combination of fear, physical force, disapproval and sarcasm. Yet what really enabled her to achieve her psychic invasion of my brothers and me was something entirely different: her vulnerability. My mother needed us. She hurt, and her anguish bound us to her.

The walk from the 102 bus stop on Falloden Way to where we lived in Brim Hill was up a steep incline so, even though it was bitterly cold, I arrived sweaty and slightly out of breath. In addition to two of my father's old leather briefcases stuffed full of homework and books, I carried my games bag, a nasty brown thing with rope straps that dug unpleasantly into my shoulders. As I approached the house I was relieved to see the car in the drive. Good, my mother was home. I rang the front doorbell and waited, panting gently, desperate to put down the heavy bags. She didn't come. I rang the bell again. Perhaps she had gone to visit her friend and confidante, Ruth Raperport, who lived around the corner. When it was clear no one was home I dumped all three bags, found my key and let myself in.

Before the door was properly open I heard the sound – a low, continuous, guttural moan – and in that moment I knew precisely how the next few hours would be spent. Leaving my bags where they had fallen, but closing the front door behind me so that we wouldn't be disturbed unexpectedly, I went directly to the kitchen. She was seated at the table, her head resting on its surface, her face turned away from me. Awkwardly I put my arms around her and tried to pull her into an upright position.

'Oh, Mum, Mum, what's wrong?'

She continued to moan. Her eyes were closed and her cheeks were sodden with tears. A large, fleshy hand, gripping a piece of wet lavatory paper, appeared from under the table and patted me. She stopped moaning and in the silence I heard the clock ticking.

Finally: 'Oh, darling, what am I going to do? What are we going to do?'

Then, as if these questions were in themselves the source of her despair, more moaning and more tears, her body rocking backwards and forwards in distress.

I stretched over the chair, embracing her back as best I could. Her brown frizzy hair was pressed against my lips – was in my mouth – so that every time I spoke I felt I was eating her. Locked in this strange position I attempted to comfort her.

'Mum, tell me what it is. What's wrong, please tell me what's wrong. I can't help if you don't tell me what the problem is. It will all be fine, just explain it to me. I am sure we can work out a solution.'

Between sobs she jerked out objections: 'You don't understand. You are only twelve. It's all over. There is nothing you can do.'

But there was something I could do. I could listen. Listen to the litany of complaints about my father; or the way she was treated at work; or her money problems; or how she had been slighted by a friend. Mostly I listened to complaints about my father.

'I have had a letter from his bloody mistress – Clara. She suggested meeting. Really, I ask you. Why did your father give her my address? The stupid man.

'Your father, despite living with that other wretched woman, is still sending me his laundry and I am still doing it. Why? Why? Why? I must be mad. The bastard.

'He is so inconsiderate of my feelings. Look at this letter about Christmas suggesting that I invite him over. I don't think that anyone was ever less sensitive to another person's needs than your father. He's selfish. I am sorry you should hear this, but better you should know so that you can try to avoid becoming the same way yourself.'

The attacks, the neglect, the belittling, the terrorising – all were symptoms of a far deeper malaise: a life spent in a state of near permanent depression. For my mother was beset by feelings of self-loathing, worthlessness, anxiety and paranoia which can only be described as grotesque.

There is no doubt in my mind that she wanted to be a kind, gentle, happy, loving mother. That, on balance, she failed to achieve this – and in failing visited so much suffering on her children – would have been a source of terrible grief to her.

A complex escape plan

There was a small boy, five or six years old, whose family had no permanent home of their own. His father was a Jewish scholar (not quite as senior as a rabbi) who conducted religious ceremonies for Jews living in communities without a synagogue. The family moved around from place to place – wherever the father thought he might be able to earn some money. They carried all their worldly possessions with them and travelled by whatever means they could manage. Mostly they walked, but occasionally they would be offered a lift in the back of a horse-drawn cart; or a railway worker would allow them to ride for free in an empty freight car. They were poor. Often the boy went hungry for days on end. Once, when the parents were desperate, they left the boy in the care of strangers who offered to feed and lodge him until his mother and father could afford to send for him. These strangers were not cruel to the boy, but they made him sleep on the floor of their butcher's shop, and they worked him hard. The boy was greatly relieved when a letter containing money finally arrived enabling him to join his family. He thought that he had been abandoned for ever. That's all I know about the boy, except that his parents fell into the habit of leaving him with strangers whenever they were without funds or whenever an opportunity presented itself. I prefer to think that the parents hated these separations but I suspect from the frequency with which they occurred that they came to look upon them as quite a convenience.

There was a girl, rather a pretty girl as it happens, with beautiful golden hair, delicate features, and lovely blue eyes. She lived on the top floor of a slum tenement with small rooms, thin walls, narrow corridors and steep staircases; a noisy, smelly place which was sweltering in summer and freezing in winter. Of her family I know nothing. There might have been a lot of them, or then again there might not, I can't say. I can tell you, however, that she had a new baby brother who was every bit as attractive as his elder sister. The girl was about seven or eight years old around the time I am describing. Her mother was always busy, or maybe she was negligent, but either way she expected the girl to stay out of her hair and mind the baby for hours on end. As a consequence of this the girl and her baby brother were usually to be found in the hallway outside the door of their apartment. There were lots of other children in the tenement and the girl had a number of particular friends who would come up and play with her. One day when the girl and these friends were all bored with hanging around in the hallway they decided to go down and play in the street. 'But,' said the girl, pointing to her sibling, 'I am not allowed to come downstairs. I must stay here and mind him.' Her friends said: 'Bring him, too.' So she did, and at some point during her descent she tripped and fell and dropped her baby brother, who was killed.

There was a large, extended Jewish family who lived in America. They were immigrants from Europe. The family had once been extremely religious but in an effort to integrate and become truly American many of its younger members had pretty much lapsed. The big holidays, such as Passover and Yom Kippur, were observed, but otherwise they rarely went to synagogue. A couple of them had gone so far as to change their names in order to sound less Jewish. Around 1940 a letter arrived for one of the older members of the family from her brother who had stayed behind in Europe.

The letter stated that the sender was being held prisoner by the Nazis and faced certain death if a sum of money wasn't sent immediately to secure his release. The sum of money was quite large. There was an accompanying note from the Nazis containing instructions on how the money was to be paid. The letter had the effect of setting them one against the other. Indeed, it created rifts in the family which took years to heal. The older generation did not question, for a moment, the veracity of the letter or the likelihood of the relative being released if the payment were made. The younger generation, who felt no sense of connection with Europe, who no longer saw themselves as being quite so Jewish and who would have to supply the cash (being more prosperous than their parents) were less certain about what should be done. Anyway, some doubted whether the Nazis could be trusted; others pointed out that there was no evidence that the sender of the letter was still alive; others still questioned the wisdom of trying to save such an old man. The arguments over whether to pay the ransom sparked off other subsidiary rows and long-held but previously unspoken grievances between different family members soon emerged. In the end, though, it was agreed that the money should be handed over. No acknowledgement was ever received from the Nazis and no word was ever again heard of the relative they had tried to rescue.

These three stories are the sum total of what my mother told me about her family. She gave me to understand that the boy who was always being left with strangers was her father; that the girl who accidentally killed the baby was her mother; and that the immigrants who received the letter from the Nazis were members of our extended American family. The fact is my mother seldom spoke of her background and what little she let slip must be treated with suspicion, since she was prone to exaggeration, if not outright invention. These stories could have nothing to do with us; they could belong to other people; she could have made them up or read them or heard them on the radio. Nevertheless, despite their doubtful provenance, I believe them. After all, they are good stories and it is better to have some personal history (though it may be assumed) than none at all.

What of my mother's own life before she came to England?

Her father, my Grandpa Jack, cuts a pathetic figure – a deeply ambitious yet spectacularly unsuccessful businessman whose only period of commercial glory was during the Great Depression when he demonstrated a talent for closing down department stores and selling off bankrupt stock. He was a man who was forever launching new, but ultimately doomed ventures; who sneaked out to see films in the afternoon when he should have been working; and who had a mysterious office in the Empire State Building from which he did who knows what. His income appears to have fluctuated dramatically. When he had money, however, Grandpa Jack believed in making a splash. Every penny had to be spent as quickly and as improvidently as possible. With undisguised awe my mother once described the excitement of moving into a large, luxurious apartment Grandpa Jack had leased during one of his relatively infrequent bursts of wealth; of the wonder she had felt as she drifted from room to room, sitting gingerly on the gold furniture, running her fingers over each surface, taking her shoes off so that she could sink her bare feet into the deep pile carpets, opening and closing the heavy, velvet drapes. There had been servants, too, who could be summoned by means of discreetly hidden bells. A far remove from the cramped, dull, rented homes where she spent most of her childhood.

By all accounts Grandpa Jack could be charming and munificent when it suited him; otherwise he was untrustworthy, neurotic, a bully, and not terribly bright. Worse, he was deceitful (he developed a habit of lying about even the most unimportant of matters) and unusually foul tempered.

I can vouch for his foul temper myself as I was on the receiving end of it the first and, so far as I remember, the only time we met. In 1963 or perhaps in 1964 (I was around four or five years old), Will and I were taken to the United States to be shown off to our American relatives. By then Grandpa Jack and Grandma Lily were being supported by my uncle Bob and were living not far from his home in a suburb of Chicago. Grandpa Jack, despite being retired, had not given up on the idea of making his fortune and kept himself frenetically busy devising various, wholly unrealistic, business schemes. That they all met with failure did not seem to lessen his resolve, nor did he appear to feel guilty about the fact that Bob was forever being called upon to bail him out. During our trip to Chicago we saw a good bit of Grandma Lily, but of Grandpa Jack there was no sign. We were staying at Bob's and although there were several family gatherings, Grandma Lily always arrived alone; Grandpa Jack's supposed work commitments keeping him occupied elsewhere. Finally, on the day before we were due to leave, it was agreed that we would visit Grandma Lily and Grandpa Jack – together – at their apartment.

If my mother had thought that by moving the scene of action to a different location she would succeed in forcing her father to spend time with us, she was mistaken. We arrived after breakfast to discover that Grandpa Jack had been called away and would not be back until the evening. Apparently unperturbed, my mother settled down to wait. We made a sortie to the local playground, but for most of that interminably long day Will and I amused ourselves in our grandmother's bedroom – irritating her by bouncing on the bed and flicking the television from channel to channel with the remote control (the like of which we had never seen before) until it was time to go and meet Grandpa Jack from the railway station.

'Is this him? Is this him? Is this him?'

My mother had parked the car so that it virtually blocked the station exit, its windows open in order that Will, who was asleep on the back seat, wouldn't get too hot. We had set off early in order to secure such an advantageous position, for my mother was concerned that otherwise we might miss Grandpa Jack in the crowd. As we leaned against the side of the car, warming ourselves in the late afternoon sun, I scanned the faces of the commuters pouring past us.

'There he is,' I shouted, not really knowing or caring, but desperate to be the one who spotted him.

'No it isn't, be patient.'

'Oh. Well, is this him?'

'No, dear.'

I was so used to thinking of Grandpa Jack as a concept that when, eventually, my mother nudged me and pointed I became confused. A tall man with thick white hair and a grey suit was pushing and shoving his way towards us. Who was he?

'Here he is,' said my mother.

'Hello, Grandpa,' I said, shyly.

He ignored me. 'There were no seats on the train,' he complained, by way of greeting.

My mother's response was to offer her cheek. He gave it a peremptory peck.

'It is disgraceful,' he continued, the formalities – clearly so far as he was concerned – over, 'I had to stand all the way.'

'Hello, Grandpa,' I began again.

'It was damn unpleasant.'

'I've drawn you a picture,' I insisted, pulling at his arm.

'Will you shut up, for God's sake?' he snarled, finally acknowledging my presence.

'Be quiet for a minute, Johnny,' my mother instructed.

My grandfather looked, with distaste, at Will sprawled on the back seat.

'I'll walk,' he said firmly.

Isn't it extraordinary that my mother persisted in the face of such enmity? Grandpa Jack could not have made his total lack of interest in her, or her offspring, more obvious. It was an absolute, outright and – presumably by the time we arrived in Chicago – ancient rejection. A lesser person than my mother would undoubtedly have been crushed to the point of debilitation. Yet she never once indicated to me that she thought her father's behaviour anything other than normal; and when he died of cancer (not long after our trip) she was inconsolable.

Grandma Lily is a considerably more enigmatic figure than her husband. My uncle Bob, my aunt Ranette, my elder brother Nick and my cousins David and Eric – the only members of our family still alive who knew Lily – have little to say about her except that she was beautiful. A certain reverence creeps into their voices when they mention this fact – as if it were an accomplishment worthy of some note. Perhaps it explains why she was the sort of person she was: intolerant of her daughter's looks; obsessed with appearances; dutiful without passion. She never worked, of course, but she was a prolific amateur artist and I have a number of her canvases: for the most part carefully executed oils featuring vases of flowers. I know that she was an enthusiastic seamstress, too, because I inherited her box of buttons – some of which are quite exquisite, being made from glass and bone china. I also know that she played bridge, for I have a silver bowl awarded to 'Lillian Rosenbloom, Handicap Winner, by the Women's Bridge League, 1962'. What else? She didn't like to be touched. She had a mania for cleanliness. She was always impeccably dressed – even when she was dying of Parkinson's disease. And she never discussed anything intimate, personal or emotional. In this regard she and Grandpa Jack must have been well matched, as Bob once explained to me:

'My parents never spoke of their feelings to each other – or to us. All conversations were about general topics. If you were happy, sad, worried, scared, angry, excited, sorry, miserable, pleased, anything – you kept it to yourself. It was like growing up in a vacuum. What is worse is that Elaine and I believed this was normal. We thought all families lived like this. It came as a shock to discover that other families actually talked to one another.'

If details about my mother's family background and upbringing are sketchy, I know even less about her life between when she left home and when I was born. She went to university – Pennsylvania State – against her father's wishes and without his financial support. She worked as a secretary to a publisher called Harry Abrams, whose wife, Nina, was to become her (and later my) most treasured friend. She married an academic called Robert Krap, made him change his name to Adams, and had a boy – my half-brother Nicholas – in 1946. She was frequently unfaithful to her husband and finally he, unable to bear her constant infidelity, left her for the wife of a man with whom she had been sleeping. As she approached her forties she found herself divorced, without a career or any real prospects, living in a small university town in upstate New York, and something of a social pariah due to her sexual exploits with the married men among her circle. By the time I was old enough to express real curiosity about this particular period, she was dead. Not that she would have told me much. The parents who couldn't show their love; the disastrous marriage; her illicit relationships – these were not things she would ever have been able to talk about.

In September 1958 my mother took her first trip overseas. She travelled by liner from New York to England and she was accompanied by Nicholas, then aged twelve.

The purpose of her journey was to marry my father, a man she barely knew, having had the briefest of affairs with him during the previous summer.

She was three months pregnant with me.

Afterwards she would talk about how difficult it would have been to be a single parent during that particular era; the stigma I would have suffered as an illegitimate child. She convinced herself that she had no alternative but to uproot herself and her son – to leave family and friends behind – and to throw herself on my father's mercy. The reality was a little different. To begin with, many years later she admitted to Nicholas that she could have prevented the pregnancy (there were contraceptives in the drawer of the cabinet next to the bed in which I was conceived). I also know she had considered an abortion (albeit an illegal one) since, in a moment of anger, she told me to count myself lucky I hadn't been terminated when she'd had the chance. Finally, she had had the option of accepting my father's offer to bring me up – his proposal being to remarry his first wife, Diana, whom he hoped would adopt me.

On the surface it would appear that my mother acted out of choice from the moment she decided to sleep with my father. Her pregnancy was a choice, her decision to give birth to me was a choice, her move to England was a choice, her marriage to a relative stranger was a choice. This implies, however, that she understood the consequences of her own actions. She didn't. Blindly, unthinkingly and at breakneck speed she charged towards the future, believing that it had to be better than her present and her past. My conception was the first stage in a complex escape plan. Her voyage across the Atlantic in the autumn of 1958 was effectively a flight. And my father, innocent of his new role, was her saviour. How odd that this new beginning should start with my mother scanning the faces of the crowd in Southampton fearful that she wouldn't recognise him.

Probably old enough to have a Bombshell

In my grandmother's house you reached the garden via the basement, which contained my grandfather, his library, his wine cellar and his batman from the First World War, Murphy.

Murphy's duties were vague. The first time my mother visited her prospective in-laws he had been acting as a sort of footman-cum-butler.

'Wait here please, madam,' he had wheezed, leaving her in the hallway and setting off with purpose (if not much speed) to the nether regions of the house in search of instructions. She had come to Brighton alone and on impulse. Confusingly, he had reappeared behind her, through the front door, and had taken her back outside and down the area steps.

'Sir Henry will see you in his study.'

Heavily pregnant, my mother had cautiously descended to my grandfather's lair.

'Ah,' said my grandfather rising politely from behind his desk, 'we meet. Peter has told me all about you. I should explain that I do not like Jews but, naturally, in your case I shall make an exception.' He rang a bell. 'Murphy will take you to the drawing room to see my wife.'

On the one afternoon each month that Louie, my father's nanny, was permitted to take off, my grandmother would sit at the bottom of the stairs and weep in despair as her two young sons, free of the only authority they recognised, ran riot.

My grandmother was a gentle, courteous and tolerant woman who found it impossible to criticise or admonish anyone – let alone her boys. She was attractive but not particularly pretty; short and plump, if not fat; and had the most beautiful pale blue eyes. She was devoted to both of her children, especially my father – the older – and believed that he was a genius. She felt very much the same way about my grandfather, Albert Henry Self, whom she had married despite the fact that he was the son of a tram conductor from Fulham and consequently beneath her.

My grandmother's brother, Great-Uncle Martin, known as Martini due to his fondness for the drink of that name, spent years researching our family tree and I believe he succeeded in tracing one branch of it back, in an unbroken line, to the Norman Conquest of 1066. Their father was Sir John Otter, one time Mayor of Brighton, and their mother was a Woodard – daughter of Nathaniel Woodard. The achievements of the Otters and the Woodards – here a bishopric, there the founding of a school – were recounted to me as I was growing up in such a way as to make me feel that I belonged to an ancient and distinguished dynasty. My grandmother's house in Brighton was a monument to their pre-eminence: gold-framed portraits, silver salvers bearing coats of arms, testimonial gifts from grateful members of the public – all helping to create the erroneous impression that the family was 'important'. Later I came to realise that none of my ancestors had managed to earn themselves so much as a footnote in the history books, and that my grandmother and Uncle Martini were guilty of over-romanticising their past. It was done, incidentally, without any hint of boastfulness or bragging. My grandmother was a naturally modest woman incapable of showing off. Nevertheless, she possessed the unshakeable confidence of someone born into a privileged family and thus absolutely certain of her position in society.

By 1917 my grandmother was twenty-five and her chances of marriage were deemed to be rapidly diminishing – especially as most eligible suitors had been killed in the war. So when she accepted my grandfather's proposal it was generally assumed that it was for want of a husband, any husband, rather than as a matter of choice. By the same token, my grandfather's intentions were viewed as deeply suspect. Believing him to be an adventurer, my great-grandfather wrote to his prospective son-in-law trying to put him off. More than half a century later, poking around in my grandfather's library, I found the letter he received hidden in a book. It began: 'Dear Mr Self, I understand that you intend to ask my formal consent to marry Miss Otter. Before you do so, I wish to disabuse you of any notion you may have that it will be to your pecuniary advantage,' and went on to explain that my grandmother would receive no dowry as my great-grandfather had been swindled out of his money backing 'a Jew and an Irishman' in an unspecified business venture. While my great-grandfather had indeed lost his fortune through imprudent investments, it was untrue to imply that he was impoverished as a result, or that my grandmother had no capital. In fact, a wealthy female relative supported my great-grandfather in considerable style on the strict understanding that he never again ventured into commerce; while his daughter was due to inherit a fifteen-room house in a fashionable part of Brighton. Attempts to persuade my grandfather to withdraw from the match failed; although before the wedding could take place he was forced to sign an 'Ill-advised Marriage Contract' which made it impossible for him to gain control over my grandmother's property.

As it happens, my great-grandfather's fears about his

daughter's fiancé were unfounded. My grandparents were in love, and theirs was one of the most touching and enduring relationships I have ever encountered. A few months before their silver wedding anniversary, a time by which the passion has left most marriages, my grandfather was posted to Washington to buy aeroplanes for the RAF. Both felt the separation keenly and it spawned dozens of love letters. 'Dearest Peterkins,' my grandmother wrote virtually daily, 'how I do miss you.' My grandfather replied to his 'darling Mumbles' with equal enthusiasm and tenderness. Their ardour never seemed to cool, for in my eighth year they celebrated their fiftieth wedding anniversary and I remember comparing my grandparents' obvious displays of affection towards each other with my mother's and father's constant bickering. My grandparents flirted. It was a formal, circumspect flirtation, not overtly physical, but made up of games and rituals. First thing after breakfast, for example, my grandfather would spend around ten minutes solving half the clues in the *Telegraph* crossword. My grandmother then had until lunch to complete it, with five shillings for every correct answer. The money meant nothing to either of them, and my grandmother certainly had no particular interest in crosswords. It was simply an excuse to stay in continuous contact all morning. She would interrupt my grandfather in his library with questions and requests for assistance; while he would often break off from his reading or writing to go and see how she was getting on.

My grandfather's ability to complete a crossword in a matter of minutes is a relatively minor example of his intellectual capacity. His academic achievements included eight degrees (one of which was the result of a bet with someone in his club that he could gain the qualification studying only during his daily train journey to and from London over a period of just forty weeks – selected because it was the length of an average pregnancy); books on subjects as diverse as ophthalmology and comparative religion; and his Bar examinations. By profession he was a civil servant. When my grandmother first met him (she was assigned as his driver during the First World War) he was Director of Labour at Woolwich Arsenal (despite being only twenty-six). During the Second World War he was posted to Washington by Churchill. Later his career spanned everything from Permanent Secretary at the Ministry of Civil Aviation to Chairman of the Electricity Council.

For all his accomplishments, or perhaps because of them, I would describe my grandfather as a lonely man. My grandmother's family and acquaintances remained distant, and he had little in common with his eleven brothers and sisters. He forged no personal friendships through his work: the upper echelons of the civil service were dominated by Oxbridge men and whether they refused to accept him, or whether because of his thinly disguised working-class accent he simply didn't feel comfortable with them, I do not know. He had golf and bridge partners – but none were close. He and my grandmother led a remarkably isolated existence – spending more time with servants, and former servants, than with friends. Nor, initially, can they have gained much pleasure from their children. My grandmother was barely involved in their early upbringing (my father said that being taken in to see her for fifteen minutes before tea was like visiting the Queen); while my grandfather's career and other interests meant he was largely absent from home.

At the age of seven my father was sent to boarding school at Lancing. Until this point his world had centred on his nanny, his brother and the nursery. They were a self-sufficient unit – rarely disturbed by my grandparents and for some reason never exposed to other children. Once at school, however, he began to make friends – and it was these friends who also ended up forming the nucleus of my grandparents' social life.

My father claimed he was happy at school. When you consider how young he was when he was sent away, and the treatment he suffered at the hands of both masters and boys, this is surprising. Fagging was the norm; bullying was rife; the day was long and tedious; the food was disgusting; and hundreds of seemingly pointless rules were enforced by the liberal use of corporal punishment. Survival depended on developing inner resources; becoming emotionally self-reliant and forging alliances with fellow victims. In all of these areas my father excelled, and, in particular, he developed a number of lifelong friendships.

If, as I have already mentioned, my father had problems identifying and experiencing the sensation we call love, he was partly compensated by the friendships he made – first at school, and later at university. These friendships proved themselves to be stronger than the bonds of marriage and, to a large extent, stronger than the ties of parenthood. He was as, if not more, loyal and attentive to these friends than to his wives, his mistresses and his children. He read with them; walked with them; played golf and tennis with them; debated with them; went drinking with them; entertained them; visited them; and – when they were in need – comforted and supported them. To have close friends for over seventy years seems almost unbelievable to me. Yet my father achieved this remarkable feat. Intriguingly, these friendships were not exclusive – he was pleased to share them with his family.

The house my grandmother grew up in, and eventually inherited, is still there – 16 Vernon Terrace, just off the Seven Dials in Brighton – though now (like all the houses in the street) it has been converted into flats and the private gardens opposite (once exquisitely maintained) have become a sorely neglected public park. Vernon Terrace itself is early Victorian, but it faces a charming Regency crescent in which the family had a second property, occupied by my great-grandparents. After my grandmother married she and her new husband lived in various locations before establishing themselves back at her childhood home. Over the years they moved around this substantial house, using different rooms for different purposes according to their changing requirements and moods. However, one room – the drawing room – remained untouched. Without doubt the sunniest and most pleasant room in the house, at the front it had three floor-to-ceiling windows which opened on to a narrow balcony containing an abundance of flowers and shrubs. At the back it looked out over a pretty little garden and offered views towards the South Downs. Filled with magnificent antique furniture, it had two substantial marble fireplaces and the walls were hung with fine oils and watercolours. It was here that my grandmother spent much of her day. After breakfast she would settle down at an ornate desk positioned by one of the larger windows and deal with her correspondence, instruct the cook, read the newspaper, and – of course – complete her half of the *Telegraph* crossword. Around eleven o'clock she would twist a little lever that rang a bell in the kitchen, and morning coffee would be served. An hour and a half later she would twist it again, and pre-lunch drinks would be served. Tea was taken in this room, at a table set up for the purpose in front of the fire; and so were pre-dinner cocktails. It was to this room that my father brought his friends.

When my grandmother died there was a debate over what would be a suitable inscription for her headstone and I unsuccessfully proposed that it should feature the recipe of her favourite cocktail. Her family nickname was Mumbles and the libation she invariably prepared for herself – and any visitors – consisted of an extraordinarily large tumbler of chilled gin, over which a Martini bottle had been fleetingly waved: the resulting concoction being referred to as one of Mumbles's Bombshells. It lived up to its name: almost instant intoxication was inevitable for all but the most hardened of drinkers. Her liberality with the gin extended to the age of those to whom it was served, and it is easy to understand how – on these grounds alone – she would have become popular with my father's set. I had my first Bombshell when I was thirteen.

'Johnny is probably old enough to have a Bombshell.' My grandmother was busy chilling the gin.

'Well, a small one,' my father replied absently, munching on a handful of 'bits' (the salted crackers and nuts which were part of my grandmother's drinking ritual).

'It'll do you good, Johnny,' one of them is sure to have said to me, because virtually anything any of us felt like doing was immediately vested with health-giving qualities.

'I'm going to skip school and stay in bed.'

'It'll do you good.'

'I think I'll have another cigarette.'

'It'll do you good.'

'I'm having an affair with a married woman.'

'It'll do you good.'

It was typical of my grandmother that she never passed judgement on any action taken by a member of her close family. If she disapproved or was in any way distressed, she kept it to herself, with the single and puzzling exception of my son Nathaniel's christening, about which she became obsessive.

'I really wish you would get him baptised.'

All conversations sooner or later took this particular turn.

'It would be hypocritical of me, Granny.'

'It's not fair on him. If he were to die he would end up in Limbo.'

'Even if I agreed, his mother wouldn't let me.'

'Couldn't you arrange it without her knowing?'

'That would be terrible.'

'Limbo is a dreadful place. All those poor children. Stuck.'

'He'll have to take his chances.'

'Colin could do it for you and Jo would be none the wiser.'
Colin MacGregor, an old schoolfriend of my father, was a
vicar.

'I am sorry, I can't. It wouldn't be right.'

'I wish I could persuade you. Oh, well. Have another
Bombshell.'

In addition to pressing copious quantities of drink (and
food) on to her guests, my grandmother encouraged them to
engage in a variety of different games. Children got to play a
Victorian board game called Willy's Walk to Grandmama, as
well as snakes and ladders, foxes and geese, and tiddlywinks.
Older guests played backgammon, chess or bezique. In
summer, regardless of your age, you could easily find yourself
being herded outside for cricket or piggy in the middle. She
was an exemplary hostess, and had the knack of putting
everyone at their ease; listening with genuine interest to what
each guest had to say, and creating the impression that she felt
honoured to be the recipient of their company. Little wonder,
then, that my father's friends should keep in touch with her
long after he left home; that they should bring their own families to visit; or that many remained in regular contact with
her until she died in 1984.

My grandfather made only the briefest of appearances at
most social gatherings, preferring to continue work on whatever project he had in hand. These projects were all absorbing
and he was capable of sitting alone in his library, thinking, for
hours on end with no apparent form of stimulation and
without having to write anything down, because his memory
was so good. Burning ambition, rigid self-discipline, a strict
moral code, immense will-power and a formidable mind –

combined, as they were, in a gigantic and athletic body – made my grandfather an imposing figure. There was a palpable sense of relief, even from my grandmother, when he left a room. He did not exert control in an obvious way: he never pressured, intimidated or demeaned anyone. Nor did he overtly (or covertly) display the slightest sign of anger or disappointment with regard to the behaviour of others. Perhaps – given that he participated so infrequently in family life – it was the fear of being ignored and neglected which kept those around him in check. At any rate, the force of his personality was such that he dominated his wife, his children and his servants.

When my father and my uncle became teenagers they began to see more of their parents. Louie, their nanny, was still employed to look after them – but now they ate in the dining room and not in the nursery. The pattern of these meals never changed. Breakfast was a massive affair: the sideboard covered with dishes containing eggs, bacon, sausages, kippers, haddock, tomatoes, mushrooms, porridge and toast; the table laid with silver, linen and crystal. Lunch was equally formal – the main meal of the day. In the afternoon a high tea was served, but – since there was rarely anyone to entertain in the evenings – dinner was often quite light: cold meats or a pie with boiled potatoes and salad. Conversation followed a set pattern, too. As soon as grace had been said my grandfather always made what appeared, on the surface of it, to be an innocent remark about a topic of general interest. This could be on any theme from economics to religion, or from philosophy to sport, but usually he made reference to the political events of the day.

'The strike hasn't ended yet.'

Initially, the ensuing discussion would be friendly enough, although the brothers could be relied upon to adopt diametrically opposing positions on any subject. Gradually, however, they would begin to raise their voices in dissent.

'No. No. No. You are completely wrong. If you look at the evidence –'

'You don't understand, do you? The whole thrust of what I am saying is that –'

Inevitably they would begin to shout. It was an extraordinary sight to witness: my grandparents sitting impassively at either end of the table, while my father and my uncle – eyes bulging, faces red – roared incoherently at each other across the middle. Eventually my grandfather would interrupt and his sons would fall silent.

'I am not sure that either of you has taken the following facts into consideration –'

Begrudgingly, aware of the impossibility of ever refuting any argument put forward by their father, they would back down. Not that defeat was ever acknowledged. Instead, after the altercation was over, the two of them developed the unnerving habit of describing the conflict in considerable detail to imaginary third parties. Each of them would stare, unseeingly, at an inanimate object on the far side of the room and would address it as if it were sympathetic to their cause.

'I said to him, "That simply isn't true," but he didn't listen to me –'

'There is no point in trying to explain it to him, he simply hasn't the mental ability to –'

It was a cycle none of the participants ever managed to break out of and it meant that the period immediately after mealtimes tended to be tense and antagonistic. Innocent bystanders, such as we children, learned to make themselves scarce until a more peaceful atmosphere prevailed.

When my father went up to Oxford there was every reason to believe that a glittering future lay before him. He was intelligent, ambitious and popular; his own father was extremely successful; and in an era when such things still mattered, he came from a good family. His plan, after university, was to enter politics. Highly principled, with a keen sense of justice, his leanings were to the left. He was a strong supporter of the Fabians and a vociferous critic of wealth and inequality. Since he found it easy to pass exams he had plenty of time to devote to his other interests. He and his friends formed a club called the Carr Society – named after John Carr, the detective writer – membership of which entailed long country rambles, even longer drinking sessions and the telling of 'whodunnits'. He became a voracious reader, joined debating groups, played tennis, punted on the Thames, and – during his holidays – went on walking tours. It was in many respects the most idyllic period of my father's life – overflowing with potential, untouched by disappointment, and free from the need to make any decisions.

My father found it difficult to make decisions. The process was slow and painful to witness, involving, as it did, a repeated analysis of the advantages and disadvantages of each possible course of action. Once made, he frequently regretted whatever option he had plumped for, and his speech was often punctuated with the words 'if only I had'.

The advent of war brought him face to face with a particularly thorny decision: should he join up? It is easy to imagine him, barely twenty years old, passionately discussing what he would have called 'the pros and cons of the issue' with his friends at Oxford.

'On one hand,' he would have said, 'I believe that it is fundamentally wrong forcibly to end another human life. Life is sacred. It is only for God to give life or to take it away.'

My father had a slightly pious streak.

'On the other hand, we are threatened with invasion, and it may be a case of kill or be killed. I have a responsibility to my family and my countrymen.'

He vacillated wildly between the alternatives – and might have continued thus until the end of the war had he not been

51

forced, by law, to enrol for conscription before 31 December 1939. Waiting until the last possible moment, he finally declared himself a pacifist and applied for Conscientious Objector – or CO – status; which was granted to him by Reading Tribunal in early 1940. Officially my father became registered for conditional service – and as such could have been compelled to perform any war work that was not in direct conflict with his principles. In practice he was free, for the duration, to do whatever he wanted.

There was a wartime recruitment poster of a pretty little girl sitting on a man's knee with the headline: 'What did you do in the war, Daddy?' I remember coming across it in a history book when I was about twelve or thirteen, and realising that it was not a question I could ever ask my father. I knew, of course, that he had chosen not to fight and that it was a mistake to mention it at school, as another boy had been teased because his father was a 'dirty conchie'. I knew, too, that my mother thought less of him for it: 'How could you not have seen that Hitler was an evil man? Were you blind? Or was it that you were scared?'

My father often argued that no one in Britain had realised what Hitler was doing to the Jews, but I never heard him argue that he wasn't afraid. At the time he and his friends had joked: 'Just because we are Conscientious Objectors, and coincidentally cowards, does not mean the two facts are connected.'

Was it braver to have taken a moral stand in the face of overwhelming opposition, to have invited the criticism and contempt of almost everyone you met, always to have wondered if you were acting on principle or because you feared for your own safety, than it would have been to risk injury or death in the armed forces? If my father had thrown himself into the war effort this question would probably not matter. As it was, he finished his degree; received a first; spent a

52

summer working on a farm; and then got a job writing for *The Economist*; a course of action which left his true motivations unclear, both to himself and to everyone else.

My father discovered girls so late in life that they should, by all rights, be referred to as women. He claimed that he didn't have any opportunity to meet the opposite sex until he was well into his twenties – and it is true that his parents' lack of a social life, the cloistered atmosphere of Lancing, and the gender imbalance at Oxford meant that he didn't come into contact with many females of the right age. On the other hand, he was averse to change and, broadly speaking, closed to new experiences. At eighteen, for example, his anxiety about going to university was such that, despite having won an Exhibition to Balliol, he stayed on at school for an extra year. In the same way, he was nervous about swapping the society of men for the society of women – though once he had conquered this fear, there was no holding him back.

Stories of my father's womanising are legion and he was still at it until his death. Aged seventy-eight he announced to me that he was thinking of getting married again.

'That's romantic,' I opined, 'who have you fallen in love with?'

'Well, to be candid, dear boy, there is a choice of three.'

Yet it would be wrong to brand him as a philanderer. He just got lonely.

'I don't know how you can bear to be alone in that big house of yours for seven whole days,' he once admitted to me when I explained that I was spending a week entirely by myself, 'I should require company.'

This craving for company led to several long-term relationships. My mother, who became the second Mrs Peter Self, befriended him while he was away from home on an extended lecture tour; the third Mrs Peter Self did much the same thing, with the ironic difference that it was my mother who was away from home on an extended trip; and several of his other romances began in similar circumstances. The fact was, leave my father to his own devices for more than a day or two, and his instinct was to seek out the society of women.

When I got to know her in my late teens I began to wish that my father's first wife – Diana – had been my mother. She had so many qualities that my own mother lacked: emotional stability, warmth of character, honesty and wisdom. More than this, she was stylish, graceful, witty and undeniably good looking.

Within hours of Diana starting work at *The Economist* in spring 1950, my father, with unusual decisiveness, rang Colin MacGregor and announced, breathlessly: 'I know who I am going to marry.'

Six months later he did. But before he could woo Diana he had to end his first proper affair. The woman concerned was a young divorcee called Sandra Moiseiwitsch, about whom my father had already said to Colin: 'I can imagine her as a mistress, but not as a wife.' Sandra did not, however, recede into the background after my father dropped her. Instead, as my mother put it, she became like Banquo's ghost and appeared at all our important family gatherings – though whether this induced even a mild sense of guilt in my father would be a moot point. Perhaps it is not surprising she came to all the weddings, funerals, christenings and anniversaries, since her half-sister – Penny – married my father's brother in 1951.

My father and his brother were motivated by overwhelming feelings of rivalry. I do not see it as a coincidence that my uncle Michael married Penny soon after my father married Diana. While there is definitely a direct connection between Penny becoming pregnant in 1956 and the end of what was otherwise a successful marriage between my father and Diana in 1957. He was eaten up with jealousy that his younger brother should have beaten him to parenthood – even if he had only had a daughter. My father could think and speak of nothing else until Diana, unable to deal with the pressure he was putting on her, left him and moved to New York to become *The Economist*'s US correspondent. The following year my father also went to America – ostensibly on a lecture tour. There he met my mother and unwittingly manoeuvred himself back to first place ahead of his brother, by begetting a son.

Mrs Mac, have you stolen my underwear?

An autumn day in 1966.

Will and I are in our bedroom. My mother is preparing afternoon tea for some of my father's foreign students who are expected at any moment. They are travelling to us as a group, by public transport, and have been given instructions on how to walk to our house from the nearest Tube station, which is East Finchley. All my father's foreign students are invited to Sunday afternoon tea at least once during the academic year. Usually they are shy, and understand very little English, so their visits are awkward. My mother makes a great fuss of them and speaks slowly and carefully, enunciating every syllable. She endeavours to discover what each student is doing over the Christmas holiday. If they have nowhere definite to go they will be pressed into joining us for Christmas lunch.

The house is quiet. I am looking out of the window, watching for the students. The man over the road is washing his car.

Without any warning there is a commotion downstairs. Voices are raised. The front door is slammed. My mother is shouting something at my father, who is banging on the drawing room window to be let back in. He gets some rocks and begins to smash individual panes of glass. As each pane breaks there is a loud popping sound. This is happening right underneath me, but I don't look down. Instead, I concentrate hard on the man over the road. I am anxious that the students may arrive at any moment and discover my parents fighting. The man over the road completely ignores the ruckus coming from our house, and begins to hose off the suds. My father is dancing about the front garden growling to himself one moment, bellowing at my mother the next.

'You bloody . . . you bloody,' he hesitates before using too strong a profanity and then decides that the occasion warrants it, 'you bloody bitch. I have cut myself. It is your fault. I am bleeding. I am bleeding to death.'

My mother lets him in. There is still no sign of the students. I feel desperately tense. Will says something to me.

'Shut up,' I snap back.

'Johnny, come here immediately, I need you,' my mother calls.

I rush downstairs.

'Help me,' she says. The tea things had been set out prettily under the windows which my father has broken. Now there is earth and glass in the cups, and smears of blood on the plates where he must have reached inside. My mother and I work frantically and in complete unison. Instinctively I know precisely what she wants me to do. She carries, I sweep; she washes, I dry. We move backwards and forwards between kitchen and drawing room in a strange, silent pas de deux, flowing around my father, who stands stock still in the middle of the hallway, attempting feebly to bandage his hands. I am just finishing off with the dustpan and brush when Will shouts from upstairs: 'They are here.'

'We have had a bit of an accident,' explains my mother, lightly, as she welcomes the students. My father scowls.

My parents' rows were spectacular. They were long; they were loud; and they could be violent. They were the backdrop against which my childhood took place, the constant. Wherever we were as a family, whatever we were doing, sooner or later my parents could be relied upon to quarrel. The core of the problem was that my mother did not really like my father. Every single thing he did infuriated her – even if she had asked him to do it in the first place.

'Why didn't you come straight home when you knew I needed the car?' 'Why do you always leave your coffee cups in the garden for me to bring in?' 'You know I can't bear them. You shouldn't have invited them over.' 'You are late.' 'You snore. I can't sleep.' 'You don't bathe often enough.' 'You never do anything about the house.' 'There's no point in you washing up. You do it so badly I always have to do it again.' 'You are so slow.' 'You leave your foot on the clutch when you accelerate.'

From what he read to his taste in clothes, from his sense of humour to his choice of friends – but, especially, in the manner he treated her – he could do nothing right. He responded to this litany of complaint in a variety of ways.

His core strategy was to ignore it. There could be the most awful atmosphere in the house, my mother crashing and banging in the kitchen, swearing that she had never met such a bastard in her life, and my father would be found placidly reading one room away, as if he hadn't a care in the world. A second strategy was to apologise meekly and to try to make amends. Appeasement tended to worsen my mother's temper, but my father had an equable nature and he would attempt to pacify her by promising not to repeat the offence or by immediately performing what he imagined was the desired action. He was wasting his time. It was almost impossible to placate my mother when she was angry. The final strategy was simply to remove himself completely from her ambit. This did not, of course, in any way mollify her; but did provide him with, albeit temporary, respite.

The real problem was that she wanted to fight, and he didn't. She taunted, provoked and criticised him until, worn down, he would dare to contradict her. His rebuke might be mild – 'I think you are being unfair' – but it would be sufficient excuse for her to launch a more aggressive attack.

Bickering would turn to shouting; shouting to screaming; screaming to throwing things. My mother would abandon all self-control. If my father came within striking distance, she would bite and scratch. Once I saw her smash a jug of orange juice over his head. It is extraordinary, now I come to think of it, that she never inflicted a serious wound on him.

Their rows had different endings. One of them might storm off – possibly taking the car and disappearing for several hours. Alternatively there could be a long period of sulking, during which time neither would speak to the other. It was not unknown for them to stop suddenly in the middle of the conflict and simply carry on as if nothing had occurred. One thing was certain, no matter how fierce the battle, afterwards both of them would play it down: 'It is only a small difference of opinion, boys, there is no cause for you to worry'; 'We have had a little disagreement, but it is all sorted out now.'

One of the innumerable topics over which my mother castigated my father was the lack of attention he paid to his children. He virtually ignored his stepson, Nicholas, and quickly persuaded my mother to send him away to boarding school. As to Will and me, it would be unfair to say he did nothing, but he didn't inconvenience himself much on our account and was not eager to alter his plans in order to accommodate our needs. He never fed us, bathed us, dressed us, comforted us, or – for that matter – got down on the floor and played with us. So far as I can remember he never even smacked us. Indeed, there was barely any physical contact at all. The hated kiss on the cheek and a light hug, perhaps, but no cuddling or romping. Nevertheless, it is ironic that my mother should have accused him of neglecting us, since she actively discouraged him from taking any sort of a role in our upbringing. She missed no available opportunity to exclude him, and, while he may not have been overly enthusiastic in the first place, whenever he did show any inclination to participate in our care, she firmly (or, perhaps it would be truer to say, hysterically) pushed him away. We were her sole domain; her hostages to a lasting marriage; and though she may have whinged continually about the trouble we caused her, she guarded us jealously.

At its most fundamental level my father's life remained unchanged by parenthood. He was always busy – absorbed by his career and his writing, his friends and his leisure interests. That is not to say that he didn't take his family obligations seriously – but we were allotted a certain amount of time and no more. As I grew older I became increasingly critical and did not want to be in his company, so that by the time I was eleven or twelve it had to be forced upon me. Whether I despised him more because my mother taught me to do so, or more because of his behaviour towards me, I find hard to judge.

Sunday morning at eleven-thirty Mr Wein, our next-door neighbour, would carefully reverse his car on to the street and impatiently honk the horn to summon his family for their weekly outing. They always went to the same place, Heathrow Airport, and did the same thing, had lunch and watched the planes. Although Mr Wein terrified me (he was a sour-looking man with a sharp tongue who ran a discount shop in Kentish Town called Lewmar's), I secretly longed for an invitation to accompany them. Disappointingly my mother sneered at the Weins, and in particular at their Sunday entertainment, so out of loyalty I was bound to support her.

'I don't know how you can bear going to Heathrow Airport again,' I would remark in a superior manner to Anne, their only child, 'it won't stretch your mind.' She was three or four years older than me – an unhappy, overweight girl who had been adopted, and was expected to be grateful for the fact. 'You should count yourself lucky,' Mrs Wein was forever shrieking at her, 'there are a thousand girls who would like to be in your shoes.' Whether this was the case, given the severity of conditions in the Wein household, is doubtful, but at any rate Anne appreciated their Sunday trips.

'I don't want my mind stretched,' she would explain to me with absolute conviction, 'I want to go to the airport. You get a really good meal out there, Dad buys me some sweets, and we see all the planes taking off and landing. Better than any silly old museum.'

Anne spoke these last words with some feeling, for once or twice she had been inveigled by my mother (and against her own better judgement) to accompany us on one of our Sunday expeditions.

By preference my mother devoted Sundays to the pursuit of culture. She liked to begin the day with the review sections of the *Observer* and the *Sunday Times* over an early breakfast, and to end it with what she referred to as 'my concert'. The latter took place every Sunday night in the Conway Hall, a bleak public building in Red Lion Square. The programme was devoted to chamber music and, on the one occasion when I was permitted to attend, the audience barely outnumbered the performers. The combination of a little-known venue and a poorly supported event appealed strongly to my mother's sense of inverted snobbery. She felt sorry for the musicians, too, and had convinced herself that they noticed when she failed to turn up. From teatime onwards on a Sunday she would become anxious. 'I can't miss my concert. They would be terribly let down.'

The audience mostly consisted of the same group of people each week, and though my mother never conversed with any of them, on her return she would speak breathlessly of their doings as if they were old friends of the family. I would ask her for the latest news.

'The man with the limp?'

'The man with the limp brought a young woman with him this week, I expect it was his daughter.'

'What was she like?'

'A nice-looking girl, though she had a bit of a cough.'

'And the woman with the hat?'

'The woman with the hat wasn't there again. I wonder if the organisers have her address. Perhaps I should check nothing has happened to her.'

Between reading about the arts, and attending her concert, my mother liked to see things. There wasn't a place of interest in the London area that we didn't visit. During my early years I gained an intimate working knowledge of the major museums and galleries – and was broadly familiar with all the stately homes, ancient monuments, famous gardens, historic ruins, notable churches and even important battle sites within a fifty-mile radius of our house. Her real obsession lay with the obscure, the unfashionable and the elusive. How delighted she was to learn that the Police College at Hendon had a small display of souvenirs which could only be viewed on the first Sunday afternoon of each month; or to discover that there was a permanent exhibition of nineteenth-century photography in Chelmsford Town Hall (admission 6*d*). While the Weins gorged themselves on the pleasures of Heathrow, my mother would be driving us to such destinations as Wapping or Wilmington, Nazeing or Aylesbury. Each trip was marked by the purchase of half a dozen postcards which she stored in shoeboxes at the back of her wardrobe. There hundreds of our Sundays lay, undisturbed for years, smelling of mothballs, talcum powder and leather, until she died and I gave them all away.

How we spent our Sundays – how we spent Saturdays, too, for that matter – was really determined by where we were. My mother was better able to dominate my father – and thus to control events – when we were in London. When we were in Brighton the opposite was true. Either my grandmother held a greater sway over him or imbued him with some sort of inner strength, because he was considerably more assertive when we stayed in her house. For this reason my mother probably regretted agreeing to alternate weekends at 16 Vernon Terrace. She enjoyed the status of having two homes, and our apartment in my grandmother's house was certainly larger and grander than our three-bedroomed semi-detached in London. She delighted, too, in being able to use my grand-parents' titles and the words 'Sir Henry' and 'Lady Self' could obviously be dropped into conversation more often as a result of seeing them every fortnight. But she was the least impor-tant member of the household in Brighton – marginally higher up in the pecking order than the old retainers (Doris the cook, Murphy the gardener and Mrs Doyle the house-keeper) but definitely below her own children – and her normal patterns of behaviour would certainly not have been tolerated. She was excluded, or excluded herself, from most of the activities.

My father was at his best – as a father – when I was between the ages of three and ten. Three was probably the first point at which he could hold a reasonable conversation with me, making it possible for him to pass more than a few moments in my company without being bored. By the time I was ten he began to stay away from home and, anyway, my disenchant-ment with him had set in. In 1961 we moved from The Grove in Highgate to 43 Brim Hill, and the earliest memory I have of my father is climbing into his bed at the new house so that he could tell me stories. He was a remarkably gifted and imag-inative storyteller and I only wish he had spent longer explaining how Alfred (the ambidextrous ape) escaped from the zoo, or how Horatio (the fearless boy space explorer) outsmarted the aliens.

My father was not exactly sporty, but he was active. He walked for at least an hour every day and once my legs were long enough to maintain a decent pace (he was intolerant of dawdlers) he would press me to accompany him. He also gave me rudimentary coaching in tennis and some swimming lessons. What was really important to him, however, was golf. It had been central to his relationship with his own father and not surprisingly he was keen that I should share his passion. Almost as soon as I could walk any distance I would be taken 'for a few holes' or to improve my putting. I was the unenthusiastic recipient of a set of cut-down clubs with which to practice. Once I was stronger I was enlisted to caddie for him and given lessons by a pro. Occasionally we went to a driving range to work on my swing.

Golf was basically what we did when we were in Brighton.

There were other diversions. We played on the old penny slot machines – What the Butler Saw and The Haunted House at the Palace Pier. We went ten-pin bowling. We travelled on Volk's Electric Railway. We walked along the top of the Downs, descending to the Shepherd & Dog in Fulking for lunch. We watched Sussex play cricket. But all these pastimes pale into insignificance when I think of the hours and hours we spent with my father, grandfather, uncle Mike and cousin Susie at the West Hove Golf Course.

'You will remember that lunch is at one,' my grandmother would plead as her husband, two sons and three grandchildren set off after breakfast for a morning's golf.

'We won't be late.'

'You promise?'

'We'll be back at one-thirty.'

'One. Lunch will be at one.'

'Perhaps you had better make it one-thirty to be on the safe side.'

'Very well, dear.'

It would be two, two-thirty, maybe even three o'clock before the golf party returned, hungry and tired, to face my grandmother.

'I think you might have telephoned,' she would suggest tentatively.

'Sorry.'

'Well, you are naughty,' she would admonish them mildly, ringing the bell for Doris to bring in the soup.

The topic at lunch would be the game. That they had analysed – and argued about – each stroke while they had been on the course, afterwards at the bar, and then in the car coming home in no way diminished my father's and his brother's desire to demonstrate that they were the better player.

Accusations would fly: 'Are you sure, Batface, that you didn't take an extra shot on the fourth?'

'Certain. More to the question, is your own memory reliable with regard to the seventh?'

My grandfather would smile serenely and sip his Guinness. His shirts were handmade for him with one sleeve substantially wider than the other in order to accommodate the extra muscle he had developed specifically for the purpose of hitting the ball harder and thus further. He had the satisfaction of knowing that even though he was in his late seventies he was still a formidable player who could well afford to give away shots to his two sons.

We children were desperately glad to be back home. West Hove Golf Course was exceptionally hilly and, being on the coast, during the winter high winds made it bitterly cold. There was little fun to be had in pulling heavy bags of golf clubs around for three hours, nor in hanging about outside the clubhouse (we weren't allowed inside) while the grown-ups sat in the bar. The only compensation, as far as I was concerned, was the fact that my father was prone to leaving sweets – and his loose change – in the zipper compartment of his golf bag. I expended considerable effort on stealing both items when he wasn't looking.

I stole a lot of money from my parents as a child and became quite adept at it.

My mother kept her cash in an old-fashioned leather purse with a large gilt clasp. She was casual about money; banknotes and loose change were stuffed in together with shopping lists, bills and till receipts. This made the task of removing coins much harder since I never knew quite where they were in the purse, and the slightest slip could result in a tell-tale clinking sound reaching my mother's ears. The purse itself had no particular home and when I got back from school each afternoon the first thing I did was to try to ascertain its location. Sometimes I found it immediately – sticking out of her handbag or perched on top of the fridge. Other times it would be hidden away – behind a pile of books or in among the laundry. The worst possible place for her to put it was in the chest of drawers in the hallway. This chest had metal handles which rattled noisily if you so much as brushed against them and the drawers also stuck. Consequently it was impossible to open without being heard by everyone in the house. My heart always sank when I realised that the purse was in the chest.

I rushed through the hall into the lavatory, knocking against the chest on purpose, and in the process surreptitiously opening the most likely drawer.

'Lift the seat. How many times have I got to tell you? Lift the seat.'

My mother was in the kitchen, preparing supper, not three feet away from the chest, but unable to see it. Mechanically I lifted the seat and considered my next move.

'Good boy.'

I had recognised a corner of the purse as I had opened the drawer and I was faced with a dilemma: remove the purse to a safe distance where money could be extracted with relative impunity, but with the risk that my mother would see the open drawer and realise what I was doing; or attempt to take the money out in situ, under the very nose of the enemy. Daringly I decided on the latter course of action and after pulling hard on the chain I pretended to run back through the hall, stopping almost immediately by the chest. My mother was listening to Radio Four.

'Tell your brother supper is nearly ready,' she called, not realising that I was standing so close to her.

I gently prised the clasp apart and began to feel for coins. Two shillings. Brilliant. I slid it out and dropped it into the side pocket of my shorts. Another two shillings. I slipped this into a different pocket so that it wouldn't knock against the other coin. A sixpence. I popped the coin into my mouth and, holding the purse tightly so that nothing could move around inside, eased the clasp shut and placed it back in the drawer.

'Suppertime!'

My mother's voice was so loud that I started guiltily assuming that she had come out of the kitchen and was standing next to me. I looked up expecting confrontation, but simultaneously I heard her banging pots in the sink and realised that I was safe. Nipping into the drawing room, I pushed the money behind a framed photograph on the mantelpiece, and headed back towards the kitchen. As I passed the chest I banged against it for a second time, making the handles chatter ('he stole four and six, he stole four and six'), and giving me an opportunity to close the drawer containing the purse.

'Klutz,' remarked my mother as I sat down, 'in a space of five minutes you have knocked into the chest twice.'

Stealing from my father was much easier, though he was less dependable as a source of income, since he usually came home after I was in bed and asleep. It was his habit when he got back early to change out of his suit and into a pair of Oxford bags (loose, grey, scratchy wool trousers which had been the height of fashion when he was at university in the 1930s), dumping his wallet and any money in his pockets on to the most convenient available surface in the process. All I had to do was wait until the coast was clear and simply help myself, safe in the knowledge that, no matter how much I took, it was extremely unlikely that my father would notice. I knew, anyway, that if he did become suspicious, a statement that he had been robbed would not be treated seriously. He was forever accusing members of the household of pinching his things.

'Mrs Mac, have you stolen my underwear?'

My father stood at the top of the stairs without any clothes on, a towel draped around his waist. Mrs Mac, our ancient and morose cleaner, was glaring up at him from the bottom of the stairs with a look of pained horror on her face. Before she could reply my mother's voice cut in.

'Don't be so stupid, Peter. What would Mrs Mac want with your horrid string underwear? Get a grip and try the airing cupboard.'

'The airing cupboard,' he echoed doubtfully. There was a moment's silence while he went to search.

'How did it get there?' he marvelled, domestic arrangements inducing in him a greater sense of wonder than any philosophical or religious question. He would argue with certainty about the existence of God, but the presence of his vests in the airing cupboard struck him as profoundly mysterious. Anyway, given his propensity to blame others for the loss of anything he couldn't find, it isn't surprising that when he said he was missing, say, ten shillings no one paid him the slightest attention. It was simply one in a long line of similar claims.

'Alison, I must ask you quite seriously, and for a second time, have you purloined my tweed cap?' 'Have you boys been pilfering my socks?' 'Has somebody been snaffling my change?'

On each occasion it would be assumed that he simply hadn't looked properly. I could lift as much as a pound a day from my father with impunity.

If you study photographs of me when I was quite young you'll see that before the age of seven I was desperately thin. After that I began to get heavier and heavier until, by my teens, even the kindest of observers would have had to describe me as fat. It wasn't for lack of exercise: far from it, I walked or cycled several miles a day. It was because I ate too much. On top of all the food and treats provided by my mother, I created my own, secret eating regime.

It began with a pre-breakfast expedition to buy sweets, funded by whatever money I had managed to steal the night before. I had trained myself to wake up early, between five-thirty and six-thirty, without using an alarm clock. Our house had three bedrooms – two at the front and one at the back. The back bedroom was a shrine to Nick, and Will and I were forbidden (one of my mother's most used words) to go into it – though, of course, we did.

'Get out,' she would shriek if she heard us playing in there, 'that is Nick's room. If he doesn't have his own room Nick won't think that this is his home.'

The fact that he visited us infrequently, and only then for extremely short periods (preferring to spend his holidays from school elsewhere), would suggest that he felt otherwise. But under a certain amount of maternal pressure he had left a few of his personal possessions in the room: a Mexican poncho; worry beads; a ceremonial sword; a few books; some

69

jazz records; and a record player. While these items were of endless fascination to Will and me, they were clearly of little or no value to our elder brother, since he never bothered to claim them, even when Mother died. Of the two bedrooms at the front, my parents occupied the one nearest the top of the stairs, and Will and I unenthusiastically shared the other.

The moment I opened my eyes each morning my first thought was always about how I would get out of the house without being heard, and as I pulled my clothes on over my pyjamas I would weigh up the advantages and disadvantages of each option. In every respect the layout and designated use of the upstairs were against me. Will was a light sleeper and the threat of his waking predicated against the most obvious route: straight out of the window. To exit by this means all I had to do was remove some child-restraint bars which my mother thought were firmly screwed in, but which I had carefully loosened some time previously; lower myself on to a small ledge; and then shimmy down the drainpipe. Creeping through the hallway and down the stairs wouldn't disturb Will – but was infinitely more dangerous so far as my parents were concerned. The floorboards and the stair treads creaked noisily; and I had to pass their bedroom door, which, infuriatingly, they always left open. Notwithstanding these hazards, I can report that I never once failed to reach the relative safety of the street undetected.

The only newsagent in the area to open early enough for my purposes was located about a mile away in East End Road. Conscious that I needed to be back in the house by seven-fifteen at the latest, a good half-hour before my parents generally rose, I would jog there – along Brim Hill and up Ossulton Way. As I ran I would plan my purchases, considering the benefits and cost of the various alternatives (I knew the exact price of everything in which I was interested) so that when I arrived – hot and out of breath – I was able to make my selection without hesitation. Not only did I have to get back home before my absence was noticed, but I also needed at least half an hour to consume what I had bought. For this reason I stuck largely to soft, easily devoured sweets such as jelly babies and liquorice. I always walked back the long way round – through Abbots Gardens – as there was less chance of being spotted by any of our neighbours. Another reason to return home this way was that it involved traversing two long alleyways – each lined by thick privet hedges – ideal for disposing of wrappers.

What I wanted during this period, more than anything else, was a dog. A dog would be company. A dog would provide me with an excuse to be up and about before the rest of the family, to go for long evening walks. A dog would make the ideal cover. And I needed cover. I was stealing so much money that I was having trouble spending it. I had enough cash most days to pay for pre-school sweets; sweets from the tuck shop at school; and, if I could think of an excuse to visit the local shops after I got home in the afternoon, sweets before supper.

I was ecstatic when, on my ninth birthday, I was given Brownie.

Hit him back, and hit him harder

My life as a petty criminal and secret eater led to a certain amount of isolation. When I invited Jonathan Raperport, the only boy in the neighbourhood with whom I was genuinely friendly, to accompany me one morning, he failed to steal any money; he took more than his share of sweets; and then he told on me. My mother was surprisingly pragmatic, explaining it, as she explained so much of my behaviour, as a phase. Capable of delivering the most vicious of beatings for relatively minor misdemeanours, in this instance she chose only to smack me, suggesting simultaneously that I should not do it again. I expect she said what she always said when she was in a relatively good mood, but fed up with one or other of her children: 'My nerfs, my nerfs. I am just about ready to hand in my motherhood badge.'

Relieved to have got away with so light a punishment, I determined that I should not be caught again, and after that worked alone. Once I had Brownie I needed no other excuse to be out of the house and together we explored every street, alleyway, wasteland, playground, and park within three or four miles of Brim Hill. As I walked (and ate) I dreamed of being grown up. I had a particular fantasy which involved first searching the classifieds for a job that I thought I would be able to do, and then calculating how I would spend my wages. I knew the precise cost of renting a bedsit; what to budget for food, clothes and travel; and how much I would have left over for comics and sweets.

This longing for independence was probably one of the major reasons why I had such trouble making friends at school. It was reinforced by the growing realisation that I didn't naturally fit into any specific group.

'If your mother is a Jew, you are a Jew,' pronounced Rosenbaum (first name long forgotten), showing decidedly rabbinical tendencies at the age of eleven. But if I was Jewish, why had I never been to synagogue? Why didn't we have a family meal on Friday nights? Why did my mother serve bacon? And – most damning of all – why didn't my parents mix with other Jews? 'Just because you are a Jew,' explained Rosenbaum omnisciently, 'doesn't mean you are actually Jewish.'

I was Jewish enough, though, not to feel comfortable with boys who weren't. My Christian credentials were impeccable: I had been baptised, I was descended (on my father's side) from a long line of clergymen, we went regularly to church, and my godfather was a vicar. Nevertheless, I had heard enough of the anti-Semitic cloakroom talk to know that I could never become really close with the non-Jewish boys for fear of being exposed as an impostor. There was the class issue, too. This was of critical importance to my mother who, typically, held two almost diametrically opposing views – neither of which was founded on any sort of reality.

'You are upper middle class, and don't you forget it,' she would rant, 'don't ever use words like dessert or serviette.'

Another day she would speak joyfully of our bohemian status. 'Because we are bohemian we are above class, beyond it. Class is not an issue for us. That is the wonderful thing about being members of the intelligentsia.'

Such delusions may have made her happy, but they left me confused. There were exceedingly posh people at my prep school and I knew in my heart that we did not rank among their number. Nor were we part of the Hampstead arty set. My father was a professor of public administration at the London School of Economics, not a poet like Alvarez's dad, or a painter like Smythson's mum. We weren't rich, either. Yes, we lived in the Hampstead Garden Suburb (which sounded good), but ours was a small house situated at its furthermost extreme: in East Finchley, if I was honest.

My family's eccentricities were obvious to all, and other boys were not afraid to point them out: 'Why do your parents drive a converted Post Office van?' 'Was that your mum and dad fighting outside the school gates yesterday?'; 'Self, did you see *Batman* last night? Wasn't it great when the Riddler is about to kill him and Robin smashes through the skylight and uses his . . . but I was forgetting you don't have a television, do you, Self, because your mother doesn't approve of it? Spector, Foot, did you see *Batman* last night? Wasn't it great when –'

I tried to make the most of these differences, to capitalise on them: 'I have been to fourteen different foreign countries'; 'When I grow up I can decide whether I want to be American or English'; 'I was an accident. My parents got married two weeks before I was born so I wouldn't be a bastard.' But no matter what I said, it was hard to keep the attention of the in crowd or their followers. My friends, my audience, had to be chosen from among the other misfits: McGregor, the headmaster's son; Proops, the school scapegoat; Richardson, the scholarship boy whose father was a policeman; Brown, who was always sickly.

My first school (I went there until I was seven) was called Golders Hill and was owned and run by Miss Davies – a cantankerous, elderly woman who hated children. She wore the most abrasive clothes I have ever seen in my life, a tweed suit the consistency and colour of scouring pads, thick socks with garters and what I now recognise to be a beret but which I then assumed to be a tea cosy. The pupils at her school wore a similar uniform – the worst part of which was a pair of heavy wool shorts that made you itch all summer and provided no warmth at all in winter (we were only allowed to wear long trousers if it was snowing). I started at this establishment when I was four and on my first day, when it was discovered that my mother had already taught me to read, I was taken out of kindergarten and 'put up a year' into the terrifying Miss Fishgerald's class. The school's unilateral decision on this issue infuriated my mother and she and my father had a long and inconclusive argument about it, leaving me (even now) with the lasting expectation that at any moment someone may come along and tell me that the time has arrived for me to be 'put back down'. Miss Fishgerald (that's how it sounded to me and I never called her anything else) had mysterious brown stains on her fingers (I remained sceptical about my mother's subsequent explanation that it was because Miss Fishgerald smoked) and a voice like pouring gravel. I arrived in the middle of a French lesson and I attribute my inability to grasp this (or any other) language to the confusion I felt that day.

I was driven to Golders Hill by one or other of my parents, but I was collected by Alison. She was employed as our nanny around the time Will was born, but when we were too old to need a nanny she took on other domestic functions – minding us, shopping, cooking, dog care, even light housework. For periods she was with us all day, every day. At other times she only came for an afternoon or two a week – providing a similar service for other women my mother had introduced her to. Whether working for us, or not, she was always dropping in and was – in the true meaning of the word – a friend of the family.

I owe a great deal to Alison. In a volatile household where

everything was in a perpetual state of crisis and flux, she was an oasis of calm and stability. Crucially she could be relied upon to comfort and care for me when my parents were otherwise engaged. She was unyielding, and by today's standards something of a disciplinarian, but the love and attention she provided were consistent. She instilled in me many of her own values: manners, patience, kindness, the importance of hard work and a sense of inner discipline. In direct contrast to my mother (who was devious and scheming), she was scrupulously honest.

How my mother found her, I don't know. She came before Will was born, because I can distinctly remember standing with her in our hallway at Brim Hill waiting for my parents to bring him back from the hospital. That would have been 1961 and she must have been in her early thirties. She never spoke about her life and I only learned about her past by accident.

'I was thinking it would be nice to come out with you to Australia,' she said unexpectedly not that long ago.

'That would be marvellous.'

'Just to see the place again.'

'Again?'

'Well, I am Australian.'

'Are you? If I ever knew that, I had forgotten.'

'I'm not interested in tracing my brothers and sister. Your mother always wanted me to do that. But I wouldn't have anything in common with them now.'

'I don't understand.'

'My parents were not well to do. It was a struggle for them. Of course, they thought they were doing the best thing for me. And she had never married or had children.'

'What did they do for the best? Who had never married?'

'They sent me to England to live with my mother's sister. My maiden aunt, dear.'

'How old were you?'

'Seven.'

'You went by yourself?'

'Yes.' Matter of fact, as if there were nothing unusual about a seven-year-old girl leaving her family and travelling halfway around the world on her own to live with an absolute stranger.

'Did you ever go back to Australia?'

'Oh, yes, I went back before I was twenty, trained as a nanny, and had a wonderful job. I got to ride every day. You wouldn't think it to look at me, but I was quite a good horse-woman.'

'You didn't stay?'

'No. My aunt fell ill, you see, and she didn't have anyone else. So I came back to England.'

'What happened to your brothers and sister? Are they still alive?'

'I really don't know, Johnny. We drifted apart. The point is, we wouldn't have anything in common any more. Not now.'

Alison didn't dwell on anything terrible that had happened to her. She was never angry, bitter or resentful. If she was annoyed by something, she mentioned it once, quietly, and was disinclined to discuss it further. This was in direct contrast to both my parents.

'I really can't believe the way that ghastly man behaved,' my mother said for the twentieth time. My parents were discussing which prep school I would be sent to. The choice was Highgate – where James Burleigh, my best friend from Golders Hill was going – or University College School. I had passed the entry exams to both, but the headmaster at Highgate had said something (who knows what?) to incense my mother.

'It will have to be UCS.'

'But the boy prefers Highgate.' Schooling was a subject on which my father felt strongly.

'Highgate operates a policy of racial discrimination and religious intolerance.'

'Darling, it is a religious school and all they said was that they put some percentage limits on the numbers of non-Christians they take in each year.'

'He was anti-Semitic.'

'Well, he has a funny way of showing it since there are so many Jews in his school.'

'Johnny goes to UCS.'

'I want to go to Highgate.'

'What you want has nothing to do with it,' my mother rejoined, and she was right.

My view of UCS Junior School is, of course, coloured by the fact that my main memories relate to being bullied by Simon Gavron. He missed no opportunity to pick on me.

'Self.'

'Yes?'

'Come here, Self.'

'Why?'

'Come here.'

'Leave me alone.'

'Turn sideways.'

'No.'

'Turn sideways.'

I turned sideways, shaking slightly.

'This', explained Gavron, swiftly bringing his knee up before I had a chance to move, 'is how you give someone a really bad dead leg.'

'That wasn't a very nice thing to do,' observed Foot, a large, gentle boy who was known to be dangerous if angered. But Gavron laughed and moved off to join his cronies.

I was being bullied closer to home, too, by Julian Sefton-Green, who lived a couple of doors away.

'Hit him back and hit him harder,' advised my mother.

I tried, but I lacked the necessary aggression. Anyway, Julian was less consistent in his bullying, and if I wanted to play with someone in the street my choice was limited. Apart from Julian, Jonathan Raperport (the boy who told), their respective younger sisters, Anne Wein and my brother Will, there wasn't a child within ten minutes' walk. Out of necessity we stuck together – a motley, mismatched group of disparate ages and interests who immediately dropped each other if a 'proper' friend came over, or a superior distraction presented itself.

Will and I, as it happens, had fairly busy lives and were not dependent on the neighbourhood kids for entertainment.

We were often away from home. Leaving aside my mother's day trips and the time we spent in Brighton, we went abroad every year, sometimes more than once. To keep the cost of these foreign excursions down they would be planned off-season and around university cities where my father could earn money giving lectures. I may have experienced places such as Venice and the Algarve in the wet and cold, but I loved travelling. Twice we lived overseas for an extended period: in 1963 we passed the winter in the South of France so that my father could write a book; and in 1967 we spent a year in upstate New York while he was a visiting professor at Cornell University.

There were as many distractions when we were at home. My mother believed that Will and I should make a major contribution to the running of the house and from an early age we were assigned various tasks, including laying the table for meals, preparing vegetables, rudimentary cooking, washing up, sorting out the laundry, mowing the lawn, cutting the hedges and weeding. This was on top of the cleaning, about which my mother was fanatical. Almost as soon as we could walk, Will and I were taught to hoover, dust, polish, scrub, disinfect and wash. My mother had exacting standards and it all had to be done in a particular way and in a particular order if we did not wish to incur her wrath. You could never be sure, either, when she would be overcome with the urge to clean. It was not unknown for her to decree that the house must be blitzed from top to bottom and every spot of dirt eradicated for, say, three hours, starting at eight in the evening. Simultaneously she might also decide to move some of the furniture around. No one entering a room at 43 Brim Hill could be certain that everything would be in the same position as it had been the last time they were there. Yet, for all the cleaning and rearranging which took place, she could never rid the house of its tired, unkempt, slightly neglected air.

There was an appalling scene in the kitchen

I am unsure about the chronology of certain events. In my mind they all occurred within the space of a few weeks – although each incident may have been separated by months or even years.

About the time I was eleven or twelve my father left my mother for a woman called Clara; my mother got hepatitis and spent a long time in bed; and I moved up to UCS Senior School.

I knew that my father had other girlfriends because my mother told me about them.

'Darling, you remember Luciana – the Italian woman who came to dinner?'

'Remind me.'

'She had dyed blond hair and reeked of perfume.'

'Yes.'

'Well your father has gone to stay with her in Milan.'

'Oh.'

'And I have just this moment put the telephone down on her. "Mrs Self? Mrs Self? Is that you?" she said.' My mother made a crackling noise to indicate that the line from Italy was bad. '"Mrs Self, I am begging of you . . . beseeching you . . ."' My mother attempted, not very convincingly, to imitate Luciana's accent. '"Please, I bega you, taka back your husband. I have hada enough. He is your husband, you shoulda have him." What do you think I said?'

I stared at her blankly.

'I said she was to send him back. Do you think I made the right decision, darling? I hope I did.'

On that, as on a number of other occasions, my father had been allowed to return. But moving in with Clara was clearly different. My mother broke the news to Will and me one afternoon after she had picked us up from school. She was silent all the way home, but this in itself was nothing unusual. I only became alarmed when she pulled into the drive, turned off the engine, locked all the car doors and told us not to get out.

'Your father has left me for a woman who lives in Kilburn.' She paused, and then repeated, with considerable emphasis: 'In Kilburn.'

All three of us sat in silence for a while. I wondered why it was significant that this woman lived in Kilburn. Would my mother have been less distressed if she had resided elsewhere? Or was it typical of women in Kilburn that other women's husbands went there to live with them? Either way, there was clearly something sinister about the place. Presently my mother began to discuss practical matters. She spoke at length about how poor we would be, how she would need help, how we would have to economise. I don't think Will said a word. He was probably about nine at the time. I tried to reassure her. I hugged and stroked her and told her it would all be all right. She mentioned that we would see my father on a regular basis and that she would never stand between us. Eventually she unlocked the car and we went into the house. Our telephone was on a long cable and my mother took it into the drawing room, firmly closed the door behind her, and spent the next two hours ringing around her friends. Each call followed the same pattern. She dialled. She spoke. She listened. She sobbed. She spoke again. She rang off and dialled a new number. Snatches of her conversation could be heard throughout the house.

I don't recall how Will passed the time until dinner and bed, both of which were very late that night, but I hid in the cupboard under the stairs and dreamed happily of the attention I would receive at school when everyone discovered what had happened.

I was not disappointed. Divorce was far less common in those days and children from broken homes were a decided rarity. The response from staff and pupils alike was most gratifying. As the word spread, teachers and boys I didn't even know went out of their way to pat my back and make 'bad luck, Selfy' noises. I enjoyed playing the role of a traumatised-but-plucky child soldiering on and threw everything I had into my performance. I received good notices, too. My form master asked me to stay back one evening after school.

'I have been watching you, Self.'

'Yes, sir,' I replied nervously, fearing that he knew it was all an act.

'I can see that you are making a superhuman effort not to allow what is happening at home to affect your schoolwork. I want to congratulate you and to let you know that my door is always open.'

'Thank you, sir.'

I began to consider a career on the stage.

My mother was enjoying herself every bit as much as the long-suffering wife who has been abandoned with two small children to care for. There were so many ways to react to the situation that she hardly knew which one to choose, so she chose them all. In the space of a single morning she might be: Silent But Strong – The Woman Who Always Copes; The Inconsolable Wife Who Has Lost The Only Man She Ever Loved; The Brave Mother Holding It All Together For Her Little Darlings; or Wronged Of East Finchley Who Is Not Going To Take Such Treatment Lying Down. One moment she was in despair, smashing crockery, hurling herself against the wall in her anguish; the next she was speaking calmly of how she would take her revenge and make my father suffer for what he had done to us.

In many respects their separation made little difference to my life. Though my mother spoke daily of our impending destitution and my father's meanness with money, there was no evidence to support her claims. We lived in the same house; Will and I continued to be educated at the same private schools; and we never went without food, clothes or holidays. I hadn't seen much of my father before he left, and in this regard nothing had changed. We met sporadically in restaurants and cafés. Once, when he had a bad sore throat, he asked if I would like to come over to Clara's house for the afternoon. I accepted his invitation.

My mother appeared to be relaxed when I informed her where I was going, but half an hour later she retired to bed with a migraine. She was in too much pain to give me a lift in the car, but she recovered sufficiently just before I left to issue instructions.

'Find out as much about her as you can. If you ask nicely she won't think it is rude. Not that I care. But if you are polite she will be more open. Remember, I expect a full report.'

The journey by bus was long and tedious and I amused myself by imagining that I was a spy slinking surreptitiously behind enemy lines to carry out a vital interrogation. 'So, Clara, what did your father do?' 'Tell me, how do you support yourself?' 'Is there a mortgage on this property?'

The house was sizeable, located in one of those wide, leafy Victorian avenues which run westwards from Kilburn High Road. I found it without any difficulty and while my finger was still on the bell, the front door was opened by my father, who must have been standing right behind it. It was the fastest thing I had ever seen him do and I can remember being quite taken aback. He looked in a bad way, unshaven and wan. He was wearing someone else's dressing gown and pyjamas and this struck me as being terribly sad. He gave me the usual, scratchy kiss and we descended down some narrow stairs to a dark, damp basement.

It had been my intention, out of loyalty to my mother, to remain distant and aloof during the visit. However, both Clara and my father were obviously so anxious, so concerned about making me comfortable, that I felt it incumbent upon myself to put them at their ease. I chatted away as if there was nothing in the least bit unusual about the situation, and tried to make sure that there weren't any awkward gaps in the conversation. We sat in a dingy living room and while we were talking Clara served high tea. In her nervousness she had prepared far too large a meal and my heart went out to her as she brought plate after plate of food from the kitchen.

'Do you like chocolate cake? Of course you do, all boys like chocolate cake. I hope you like biscuits? I have several different kinds. There is some jelly if you are interested. And a plate of sandwiches. Oh, and I got in some . . .'

Although my mother had never met Clara (and knew no one, other than my father, who had), this had not prevented her from describing her rival to me in considerable detail. I had been primed for a meeting with a younger woman – someone thin, attractive and glamorous – probably with a career. I was ready, too, to repel her attempts to charm me.

'She will go out of her way to flatter you, Johnny. Do not be fooled, she is Machiavellian, that one.'

So prepared was I for the Clara of my mother's imagination that for the first few minutes I believed I was meeting a different Clara. Perhaps a relative with the same name – a cousin or an aunt. The Clara in front of me was short, decidedly plump and most definitely as old (if not older) than my father. She was tense, shy, devoid of charisma and – far from having a career – had devoted her life to caring for her late parents. When I relayed this information to my mother that evening she accused me of entering into a conspiracy with my father in order to deceive her. Eventually I convinced her that I was telling the truth and the subject was dropped. The next day she began to refer to Clara as the Gnome of Kilburn.

My father's absence, far from upsetting me, brought a number of tangible benefits. My mother announced to the world that I was the man of the house, her chief adviser. No major decision was taken without my approval, or at least my input. At the same time I was granted considerable independence and (finally) given my own bedroom. These rights were further enhanced when my mother became ill and was diagnosed as having hepatitis.

There is a point when childhood ends and adulthood begins. For me it was the moment my mother's fever forced her to bed – for several months as it turned out – and she put me in charge. I had some help, of course. Alison came to check on the invalid while I was at school, did the heavy shopping, and occasionally prepared evening meals. But the other chores – housework, cooking, laundry, nursing my mother and looking after Will – fell to me. I took my responsibilities seriously, believing that the survival of our family depended on my efforts. Never had the kitchen been so clean, never had the lavatory been disinfected so often, never had my room been so tidy. Motivated by the fear that, if I failed, Will and I would be forced into a foster home – or worse still made to go and live with our father in Kilburn – I worked feverishly before leaving for school in the morning, and again when I got back in the afternoon. Far from minding these extra duties I was delighted, for they brought with them a previously unimagined level of freedom. My mother was far too sick to notice my comings and goings and I took to sneaking out at night, ostensibly to walk the dog, but in reality to practise drinking and smoking. Progress was slow (I was too timid to take more than a sip of sherry and I certainly never inhaled) but the experience was thrilling. At weekends I secretly attended discos and dances held by the local youth clubs. I purchased a number of dirty magazines from boys at school. My sweet consumption peaked. I had plenty of money to buy anything I wanted since, out of necessity, I had been granted official access to my mother's purse. Apart from the nightmare of dealing with Will, life was close to perfect.

One day Will and I were talking about our childhood and I asked him whether he thought our parents had had a favourite.

'Absolutely,' he replied, 'they preferred me.'

Considering that he, in turn, might be deluding himself, I searched for an independent witness. What did Alison think on the subject?

'After Will was born there was really only one child in the house,' she said, 'and I am afraid it wasn't you.'

My father freely acknowledged the disparity of our relative positions. 'Perhaps your mother and I were overly concerned about Will and his doings. He was terribly bright, you know.'

From an early age it was clear that my younger brother possessed the very thing which our parents set the greatest store by: an exceptionally brilliant mind. So while my father's departure and my mother's illness may have opened up a world of opportunity for me, for Will, who was used to receiving a fairly constant flow of praise and adulation, it spelled misery and neglect. The new order infuriated him and, understandably, he directed his resentment towards the only remaining figure of authority: me.

It was an explosive mix: two unsupervised, jealous brothers who were close in age, one desperately trying to exercise control, the other used to being the focus of attention, both raised on a diet of domestic violence. With shame I must

87

I have a treat in store for you

I suffered repeated sexual abuse by two of the masters at UCS Senior School for most of the three years I spent there.

Although I hated participating in these sexual acts I never spoke to anyone else about what was happening, and I willingly colluded with the masters involved to keep their abuse secret.

It was my politics and economics teacher, Mike Densham, who began the abuse. I liked Mike. His disregard for rules made him an extremely attractive figure. Discipline in his classes was lax. At least once a term he would start our lesson with the breathless announcement that he had received another warning from the headmaster:

'Sorry, chaps, but if your grades don't improve – and if we don't keep the noise down a bit – I'm for the chop. Think it through – yes, Lewis, you can think if you try – you're probably better off with me than with some other bastard. How about it? Could you work like blacks – nothing personal, Jones, you know I am not a racist – at least until the Easter hols? Pull your fingers out? For my sake?'

It was difficult to resist such a frank appeal. Especially from a master who gave us cigarettes and sometimes took us to the pub for half a pint at lunchtime.

Vomiting drunk, barely thirteen years old, I found it just as difficult to resist similar pleading when, on the last night of a school trip, he begged me to take off all my clothes and get into bed with him.

What started as, effectively, a rape continued much in the manner of an illicit affair. Mike impressed on me the need for secrecy and willingly I complied. It was all right to be seen together but there must always be a reason. He wrote to my father suggesting that I would benefit from additional tuition. He organised special outings after school. He persuaded other teachers to arrange extra-curricular events for evenings and weekends which we could both, without exciting suspicion, attend. In this way at least once a week, and sometimes twice, we were able to meet.

In the early days, although I looked much older than I was, there were only a limited number of places we could go. It came down to restaurants, pubs, a gay club in the Finchley Road, where the presence of a middle-aged man and a child drinking together late at night did not appear to arouse comment, and Mike's home. I intensely disliked the last of these options since it meant having sex with Mike in a bedroom (a drawn-out business), as opposed to in a car (short and hurried). Mike lived with his father, who was quite elderly, and my visits always seemed to commence with a quarrel.

'Father, look who I have brought home for a bit of tutoring. So that we can have the house to ourselves, why don't you go out for a drive?'

'I won't disturb you.'

'You know I prefer you to go out while I am teaching.'

'You know I prefer to stay in. I'll make some Spam sandwiches in the kitchen. He'd like some sandwiches.'

'Father, we have spoken about this before.'

'Michael, if you don't mind, I'll stay in.'

'It is rude to argue in front of a guest.'

They would leave the room. I would take a few long swigs

from one of the many bottles of spirits scattered about the sideboard. After a few minutes the front door would slam and I would hear a car starting in the street. Mike's father had gone for his drive.

Drink was pivotal to our relationship. It was important to both of us that I got drunk whenever we met. Mike haunted two particular pubs in Hampstead. In one there were frequently other couples made up of older men with younger boyfriends or girlfriends. This was a pub for hardened drinkers and I found it intimidating. The other pub was opposite a house belonging to two former UCS pupils – Alan Blaikley and Ken Howard – and at closing time Mike would cross the street and ring their doorbell in the hope of gaining admittance. Ken seemed immune to Mike's charm, but Alan could be prevailed upon to let us in for a cup of coffee or a final drink.

'Oh, it's y-y-y-y-ou, Mike,' Alan would stammer as if Mike were the last person on earth he expected to see. 'And, J-J-Jos.' My nickname in those days was Jos. 'You had better c-c-c-come in I s-s-suppose.'

When I was a little older – perhaps fourteen or fifteen – I took to dropping in on Alan alone. The friendship we developed, which now spans nearly thirty years, was the one positive thing to come out of my affair with Mike. Alan was the only person who seemed to suspect that something was wrong.

'You should be with f-f-f-friends of your own age. I'm n-n-not sure that I should really allow M-M-Mike to bring you around here. I d-d-d-don't think it is healthy you spending so m-m-much time with your elders.'

Although he always acted with the greatest propriety I continually expected Alan to make a pass at me and I was quite prepared to acquiesce. But he never did, and although it puzzled me, I was relieved. There were many acquaintances of Mike's, on the other hand, who regularly made passes.

Another former UCS pupil and drinking companion of Mike's, Basil Moss, was always kissing me and pinching my bottom; two teachers from UCS Junior School made a similar nuisance of themselves; and a second master from the senior school – Tony Ford – became so insistent that I have sex with him that in the end I gave in.

'I wouldn't keep harassing you,' he said the day I finally consented, 'but I know you have done it with Mike and it just isn't fair that you won't do it with me.'

Tony was gentler than Mike, and more amusing company, but he was selfish and stingy.

Mike didn't seem to mind me having sex with Tony while it was happening, but when it was over he became standoffish.

'How can I trust you?' he said, smiling grimly.

'You know you can trust me.'

'I'll have to think about it.'

I was wretched. I found the sex with Mike abhorrent, but I had become used to the attention, dependent on him for excitement and intrigue. In class he ignored me completely. He wouldn't even make eye contact. Out of class, no matter how I arranged things, he managed to evade me. I felt miserable, alone and rejected.

'Yes, this is Mrs Self.'

My mother had made it to the telephone first and I stood in front of her watching for a sign that the call might be for me. She and I always raced to answer the telephone. It was as if each of us was hoping for some good news that would allow us to leave home – ideally on a permanent basis.

'Oh, Mr Densham.'

I couldn't believe he was ringing my mother. I felt the blood draining from my face. What was he saying to her? What was he telling her about me?

'I see.'

Her face was impassive. She was listening intently. I moved to take the receiver from her, in the hope of ending her conversation with Mike. Impatiently she signalled me away.

'Yes. I quite understand.'

I was beside myself with fear. What was he saying?

'I will tell him. Goodbye, Mr Densham. Thank you for calling.'

'What did he want?'

'I wish you wouldn't try to interrupt me when I am on the telephone. That was your teacher, Mr Densham. An older boy has dropped out of a trip to the BBC to watch some programme or other being made. If you would like to take his place, Mr Densham will pick you up outside Baker Street Underground station at eight this evening. You must be smartly dressed, he said, but not school uniform. I take it you want to go?'

'Yes.'

'Well, you can help me clean the house this afternoon, then, before you get ready.'

I was waiting outside Baker Street long before the appointed hour, watching for the white Austin 1100 which Mike usually borrowed from his father.

'Dear boy,' he said, coming up behind me and putting his arm around my shoulder.

I jumped. 'Mike! You scared me.'

'All in a good cause. I have a treat in store for you.'

'My mother told me.'

'Not some stupid trip to the BBC. Somewhere else.'

'Where?'

'Guess.'

'How can I guess?'

'The Playboy Club.'

In the 1970s the Playboy Club was every teenage boy's fantasy. The whole country knew about the place with its scantily clad Bunny Girls who – draped in little more than a pair of rabbit ears and a velvet swimming costume – served a glamorous, jet-set clientele. It seemed the epitome of style and decadence.

'Honestly? You aren't teasing me?'

'No.'

'Gosh. But how will you get us in? Are you a member?'

'Of course.'

I stood stock still and gazed at him. He was short and dumpy, and had a round, owlish face. His hair was thinning and greasy, and his skin had an unpleasant shine to it. He wore a dirty white drip-dry shirt with a school tie, a grubby cream-coloured blazer, and grey nylon trousers with frayed bottoms. He stared back at me, his eyes glinting through the thick pebble lenses of his horn-rimmed glasses, a wolfish grin playing about his lips. Nevertheless, at that moment he seemed to me to be a giant of a man, a colossus. Someone whom I could rely upon. Someone who would look after me.

'Come on, old boy, if you want to go we'd better get a move on.'

When we arrived the doorman greeted Mike by name and all the staff seemed to expect us.

'I told them I was bringing a friend's son in to celebrate his eighteenth birthday,' Mike whispered as we waited to be seated. 'After dinner I will show you around and then I'll teach you how to play blackjack.'

I was in heaven. I was fourteen. I smoked. I drank. And now I gambled.

The lies I had to tell to keep my family, teachers and friends from discovering my secret life never caused me a second thought. My mother was forever lecturing me on the importance of truthfulness. But if it served her purpose better, she was, with her usual inconsistency, perfectly happy to condone outright falsehood. She would order me to say anything that she perceived to be to her advantage – though what constituted a valid reason for deceit could vary as wildly as her moods.

'Don't inform your father that I have a part-time job, because if you do, he will stop giving me any money and we won't have enough to live on.'

'Your brother must never, ever, know that I am buying you this new shirt. Hide it from him as soon as we get home.'

'If Ruth Hayman or anybody else calls do not say that I have gone out. You are to inform her that I am in bed with a migraine. If she comes around to see me, do not let her past the front door. I have closed the curtains in my room, incidentally, so do not open them.'

She had no compunction about lying to anyone; but she positively relished lying to those in authority. If I wanted to get out of games, or had failed to complete my homework, she delighted in the task of coming up with an appropriate excuse and virtually all of her notes to my school were works of creative fiction. A little before she died I was desperate to be released from an employment contract with a company that had bought one of my businesses. My solicitor claimed it was impossible and that I risked a long and costly legal battle if I did anything precipitous. My mother, on the other hand, came up with a number of schemes – based on absolute untruths – designed to help me manoeuvre my way out.

'Just pretend you have a serious disease. Cancer, for instance. You can hardly be expected to go on working if you don't have long to live.'

'I couldn't, Mum. Suppose I really got cancer – I'd feel I'd brought it on myself.'

'Well, a heart condition. Or a serious back problem. No one can tell with backs.'

'No, illness is out.'

'OK. Well, why not send an anonymous letter that implies

you are mounting a hostile takeover bid? They will hardly want you sitting around their offices under such circumstances. Here, I'll help you compose it now.'

My mother saw nothing immoral in what she was suggesting. As far as she was concerned the whole issue boiled down to whether I would be able to get away with it. Essentially, I grew up in an atmosphere where lying was not considered a particularly bad thing to do. What was bad was getting caught.

I never got caught.

I never even got close to being caught. My behaviour grew extreme, and still no one said anything. When I came home stoned or drunk in the small hours of the morning my mother would shout that I was being inconsiderate 'stomping around and making all that noise'. On one occasion she laughingly enquired: 'Why do you spend all your time drinking with those poofy teachers and their poofy friends? Don't think I am not aware of what is going on.'

Blushing furiously, I mumbled a response.

'Listen, it's your life. Do what you want.'

But how much she knew remained a mystery. She never raised the subject again. There was never a detailed investigation as to what I was doing when I was out of the house.

I don't think it would be an overstatement of the facts to say that I became enormously apprehensive during this period of my life. I was afraid that I would be found out; I was afraid that the sex was doing some permanent damage to my body; and I was afraid that I was gay. To overcome this last fear I became passionately interested in girls and within a year of my first encounter with Mike I found – if not exactly girl-friends – girls who would sleep with me.

What I haven't explained about the years I spent at UCS is just how busy I was. On top of my schoolwork – which was demanding – I had a large number of other interests. Every week I visited Mr Nathan (who had Parkinson's disease) and Miss Zigliotti (who was bedridden), as well as dropping in to the retirement home by the Heath to chat with the pensioners and run errands for them. I also befriended a boy called Paul, who lived in a children's home. At weekends and during the holidays I was employed by the Greater London Council as a playleader – which involved building and supervising adventure playgrounds. I started working for them when I was fourteen, and the following year I was in the bizarre position of being considered responsible enough to run a playground with two or three members of staff under me. When I was older I also helped out in a geriatric ward.

My social life, which hitherto had been almost non-existent, blossomed.

While revising for my O levels – in spring 1974 – I announced that I no longer wished to go to UCS. The reason I gave was that I did not approve of private education.

'If every MP had to send their children to a state school you can be certain the country would have a better education system,' I argued passionately.

At the time I believed in what I was saying, but looking back I realise that I was just desperate to escape from Mike's clutches.

My decision had the added benefit of irritating my father, who, as a Labour Party supporter, was – theoretically, at least – against unfair privilege. I delighted in goading him.

'Dad, you are a hypocrite. You say you are a socialist, but if you are how can you condone private education?'

He would not be drawn. 'The world isn't perfect. The only way to get a decent job is to go to a good school and on to Oxford or,' he would always take a deep breath before adding regretfully, 'at a pinch, Cambridge.'

'For years you have been telling me what sacrifices you have had to make to pay the school fees, and for years you have been threatening to take me away. Here is your chance, Dad. I want to go to a comprehensive.'

In spite of these debates, he didn't object too strongly to my switching to the state system, but Will's insistence that he wanted to do the same caused my father dreadful angst.

'Think of your brother. Effectively you'll be depriving him of a proper opportunity in life if you switch now.'

'That isn't my problem.'

'Eton is arranged on comprehensive principles. Why don't you and Will go to Eton? I wouldn't mind paying for the two of you to go there.'

'Don't make me sick.'

Meanwhile, my mother had written to inform UCS that both her children would be leaving at the end of the summer term. The school wrote back by return offering Will a completely free place for up to five years. My father was overjoyed.

'This is a turn up for the books. Think what I'll save.'

My mother was disgusted. 'They didn't even mention Johnny. The boys leave, and that's final.'

Within days it was arranged that I would go to Whitefield Comprehensive, just off the North Circular by Brent Cross. Will was enrolled for Christ's College, a grammar school located in Finchley.

Mike was devastated. 'You'll stay in touch? Say you'll stay in touch.'

'Of course I will.'

'You won't want to see me after you've left. I know you won't.'

'I will. You know I will.'

On 7 June – I remember the date because it was my father's birthday – I had sex with Mike for the last time. It was in his father's car, at one in the morning, on a side turning by the Heath Extension. I saw him once or twice after that, but his hold over me had ended.

We watched my father hurrying up and down the flickering beam of light

'I am afraid that you will have to undress me for bed.'

'That is why I am here.'

'I far prefer you undressing me to Fred.'

Fred was the person who normally looked after Francesca.

'He is so rough. And, of course, you are a real man.'

She giggled. Fred was gay.

'While you are undressing me we will continue to discuss the Ten Commandments and then you can read me another chapter of *War and Peace*. Your pronunciation of the Russian names is atrocious, but I can't fault your delivery. Which Commandment were we up to?'

'Francesca, we have never moved much beyond adultery.'

'My favourite. Nevertheless, we will switch to "Thou shalt not covet thy neighbour's wife." You will recall that during the Spanish Civil War I was evacuating children to camps in France. At the time I was in a *ménage à trois* with a man and a woman...'

I undressed her; washed her; grappled a nightie over her head; helped her on to the commode; and went to make us both some instant coffee. After a while she called that she had finished; I lifted her on to the bed; emptied and disinfected the commode; and then brought through our drinks. She produced the packet of digestives I had been searching for all day from under her pillow.

'You aren't supposed to be able to walk without assistance. How did you get those?'

'I have my methods.'

'No wonder we have mice.'

'Since you are clearly bored with your Bible lesson I will tell you about the time I was a spy.'

'Thou shalt not bear false witness?'

She ignored my interruption and leaned back on the pillows.

'I enjoyed spying. It suited my disposition. I found that the ideal way to smuggle papers and money was in a hot-water bottle . . .'

The summer I left UCS I spent six weeks in Walberswick on the Suffolk coast taking care of Francesca Wilson, by then well into her eighties. I had performed this duty the previous year, though for a shorter period, and had asked if I could do it again. Francesca had been a strong presence throughout my childhood. We had been regular guests in her Walberswick home – Creek Cottage – and we also saw a great deal of her in London. Originally she had been my father's friend (they had met when he was at Oxford, where he had dated one of her nieces), but after my parents separated, my mother had 'taken Francesca on'.

In appearance Francesca reminded one of nothing so much as a cat: sleek and sinuous. She was slender, very feminine, and always sat up straight. By the time I knew her, her hair was silvery grey, her olive skin was deeply lined, and her piercing blue eyes had begun to pale. Yet despite her age Francesca had not lost her sex appeal. She still possessed that indefinable quality which men find irresistible, and I used to tease her about the steady stream of male admirers who came to pay tribute. She flirted outrageously and she had the confidence of a woman who understands the power of her own beauty. More importantly, Francesca was sharp. She masked it with languid indifference, but she had an enquiring mind, a keen intellect (she was one of the first women to attend Cambridge) and a wicked sense of humour.

'How nice to see you,' a dull guest once exclaimed.

'Yes,' she replied, 'it must be, for you.'

Francesca was a rebel. She cared nothing for convention and took immense pleasure in any act of defiance, whether it was against the Nazis or the county council. She had a casual disregard for her personal comfort and safety and no apparent doubts or fears. She expected everything to turn out for the best, and if it didn't she was happy to adapt to circumstances. She had led the most extraordinary life and when she reminisced her stories were of White Russians and fleeing Jews, great causes and daring deeds – relating her own part in a matter-of-fact, what-else-could-one-do sort of a way that only served to make each tale all the more thrilling.

'The captain did not seem to realise it was a crisis and wanted to wait for orders from London so I was forced to commandeer his ship. I got a telegram afterwards reminding me that His Majesty's Navy was not available for my private use . . .'

'We went to all that trouble to get him out and then the British government refused to grant him refugee status, so I adopted him. I adopted quite a few refugees after that . . .'

'I got the job because I spoke Serbian. You would be surprised how few people there were in England who spoke Serbian in those days. I had learned it while on holiday there with my lover – we pretended to be cousins, you know – just after the Great War . . .'

Creek Cottage was as unorthodox as its owner. In the winter of 1960 Francesca had allowed Peter Buxton, an architect in the process of having a nervous breakdown, to stay there rent free. Come the spring he asked if he might move into the garden. Francesca agreed and he built himself a lean-to out of driftwood and old packing cases. Here he lived for the next twenty years, leaving only to tend to his allotment (thirty yards away) and to make a weekly trip to the village shop (perhaps a distance of quarter of a mile). I never knew him to bathe or shave and he always dressed in the same apparently indestructible tweed suit. Gradually he enlarged and extended the cottage, paying no heed to planning regulations and with an airy disdain for traditional building methods. The result had a decidedly temporary feel to it, and there was every reason to suppose that the whole structure was supported by the ivy he had trained throughout the interior. Even Peter admitted that his wiring and plumbing left something to be desired. The switch by the front door, for instance, operated a light in one of the upstairs bedrooms; and when you used any of the taps you couldn't be certain whether the water would run hot or cold. Peter's intense shyness – he eschewed almost all human contact – earned him the nickname Peter the Hermit and Francesca claimed that if Walberswick ever had to be evacuated again (much of it was below sea level and therefore prone to flooding) it would be women, children and hermits first.

Francesca had many friends in and around Walberswick and we led an intensely social existence. She loved to entertain and without telling me she would dispatch invitations by hand, using the next-door neighbour's children to deliver them. Returning from a walk at, say, five in the afternoon, she would greet me with the words: 'The Haycrafts may be coming for dinner.'

'What do you mean "may" be coming to dinner? Are they, or aren't they?'

'I sent a note asking them, but they haven't replied.'

'Fair enough.'

'Oh, and the Slaters may look in, too.'

'How many should I allow for?'

'Perhaps ten, if they all come. I'm afraid you will have to prepare the meal.'

So it was that, in a haphazard way, she taught me to cook. Out of sight, and barely within earshot, she would shout her instructions.

'Now, fry the onions until they are a sort of sludgy brown in colour . . .'

'What onions, Francesca? You didn't say anything about onions.'

'Didn't I? That's odd. The recipe definitely calls for onions. Never mind. Take the chops and . . .'

At the last minute I would dash around to the pub with half a dozen milk jugs to fetch beer – a locally brewed ale with a sweet, nutty taste. Guests would arrive – not necessarily the ones who were expected – and we would squeeze around a makeshift dining table for a long evening of food, drink, conversation and – if Francesca was allowed her way – word games.

'I think it would be a good idea to play Nebuchadnezzar now.'

'Oh, Francesca.'

'I will start. I am not Nebuchadnezzar, and I am not . . .'

The object of this game was to find out which well-known personality or historical character whoever was in was pretending to be. When we got bored and wanted to talk again we would foil Francesca by choosing football players.

'Grrr,' she would gnash her teeth in disgust, 'you know perfectly well that I don't know a single football player. I see you want to stop. I will have a little more to drink. Just a tear, now . . .'

Francesca hated to see an empty bed and we almost always had people staying. She gave priority to those whom she felt might not otherwise get a holiday. Accordingly there was a steady throughput of single mothers and their offspring; as well as a seemingly inexhaustible supply of artists, actors, writers and musicians. It was in this way that I met Freya Hogue, who was to become one my closest friends. An exceptionally generous woman, she had a theory about money which I have followed ever since I learned about it: 'When you lend someone money don't ask them to pay you back and don't ask for interest. Instead suggest that when they can afford to, they lend it to someone else on the same terms. In this way your money will be circulated over and over, possibly benefiting hundreds of people.'

Freya lived in a bedsit in Belsize Park, where she had a small band of enthusiastic followers, including an ex-Spitfire pilot who called himself M; a lesbian couple who swore they had been christened Hope and Charity; and one of the heirs to Castle Howard who took considerable pride in the fact that he could run his own bath and open a tin of beans without the assistance of a member of staff.

I was always happy in Walberswick and I can recall everything that ever happened to me there with perfect clarity. I can even remember my first visit to Creek Cottage in the winter of 1963. The crunch, crunch of wellington-booted feet across the shingled beach; the smell of salty wood burning in the tiny grate; the delicate taste of fresh, poached plaice; the buffeting of the wind against my body as I chased seagulls in the garden.

We arrived late at night while a gale was blowing. The electricity was down and my mother parked the car with its headlights pointing along the path to the cottage. Through the windscreen we watched my father hurrying up and down the flickering beam of light, struggling to get our boxes and bags out of the rain and safe inside. In those days the cottage was little more than a shack: a small bedroom, a living room with a galley kitchen, and a bathroom. The bedroom had two fitted bunks of painted wood and a double bed. It was heated by a paraffin stove and my parents had a long discussion about whether it would be safe to leave this on all night. In the end one of them got up and blew it out. The darkness wrapped itself about me and I felt strangely secure in its inky embrace.

In the morning, while my mother prepared breakfast, my father and I went out to explore. We climbed the bank beside the house and surveyed the scene. Whichever way we turned the most dominant feature was the sky. It towered over us – huge, translucent, impenetrable grey like a giant Tupperware bowl dropped down over the Earth. My father took me firmly by the shoulders.

'In that direction, across the marshes, lies what is left of Dunwich. A long time ago the town fell into the sea and on a still night you can hear the church bells ringing far down beneath the waves. That way, no that way, is where the railway used to . . .'

All my senses were heightened by the extremity of the place; the muted colours and the absolute desolation exhilarated me. I became conscious of the thought that I preferred the countryside to the city, that when I grew up I would lead a rural existence.

The geography of Walberswick adds considerably to its allure: meandering lanes; lush hedgerows; patchwork fields of golden wheat; mossy oak forests; open heaths with gorse and heather; hidden, reedy swamps; and a vast, duney foreshore. It is located at the most easterly point of the British Isles where the terrain is pancake flat and dips so gently into the sea that the line between what is solid and what is liquid is blurred and indistinct. Walking along the thin, stony ribbon of beach is like balancing on a tightrope; the land falling away to one side of you, the ocean to the other. If you turn your back on the vast expanse of water and look inland, the marshes stretch to the south almost as far as the eye can see;

though in the distance you may just be able to make out the green smudge of Dunwich Forest. To the west crouches the village: a huddled jumble of red-tiled roofs and pink-washed cottages clinging to the ground as if to avoid being snatched away by wind or wave. To the north, across the muddy expanse of the Blythe estuary, Southwold's whitewashed lighthouse towers over the town, the highest point for miles around.

The road to Walberswick goes nowhere else. There isn't any through traffic and it isn't served by public transport. Walberswick is an island, cut off from the rest of the world.

During the 1970s there were, perhaps, thirty or forty other teenagers who – like myself – visited Walberswick for their holidays. We divided into innumerable subgroups. At one end of the spectrum there was a strong sailing fraternity, at the other a set who passed their time slowly getting stoned. We spent our days wandering up and down the village; popping in and out of each other's houses. At lunch and in the evening we congregated in Walberswick's better pub – The Bell – which has antique wooden settles and worn flagstones that rise and fall across the floor like a gentle sea swell. Breakfast and tea found a good number of us in the village tearoom – run by a jocular woman called Mary who made mouthwatering cakes and never stopped talking. In the small hours of the morning, when the weather was fine enough, we made bonfires on the beach and swam nude. We rented rusty black bicycles from morose Mr Fisher who owned the garage; and we went riding with horses borrowed from Mrs Edwards.

I travelled as Mrs Self

Slightly drunk I stand – sway – in the pitch-black garden calling out in a hoarse, urgent whisper: 'Brownie. Brownie. Come on, you bloody dog. Brownie!'

A light snaps on. I look up and recognise my mother's nightie-clad form silhouetted against the staircase window. She peers down at me for a moment before slamming the window shut. The light goes out, plunging me back into darkness. I endeavour to call more softly.

Brownie's behaviour pretty much sums up how we all feel. She has dug an escape tunnel under the garden fence and when let out last thing at night invariably makes a bolt for it. She disappears for days on end, returning exhausted and emaciated to recuperate, before departing again. It is symptomatic of the family's malaise that no one thinks to restrain the animal. Alison, muttering ominously that the dog is being maltreated, eventually takes Brownie away to live with her.

By my sixteenth birthday my mother had given up trying to forge us into a cohesive family unit. It was patently clear that none of the participants, least of all herself, had an appetite for nuclear family life. Having arrived at this conclusion she didn't hesitate to act. If it wasn't all going to be cosy, jolly and intimate, then it had to be the opposite. With breathtaking speed and her usual decisiveness she instigated a new policy.

'From here on in you are an adult. I don't mind where you go, or what you do. All I ask is that while you continue to live under my roof you let me know you are safe, so that I don't worry.'

Meals, once the pivotal points of our day, suddenly became wholly arbitrary. Sometimes she cooked, sometimes she didn't. 'There is food in the kitchen. If you are hungry, make something.'

She stopped inviting me to do things with her. When she went out, she went alone. No more museum or gallery excursions. No more chatty restaurant meals in Hampstead. No more holidays together.

'If you are honest, Johnny, you are much happier without me interfering. The last thing you need is a mother fussing over you all the time.'

Her indifference was, of course, largely feigned. She wanted to be seen as a liberal, tolerant, free-thinking parent who had no difficulty in letting go of her baby. In reality she continued to take an obsessive, almost forensic, interest in my life.

'Don't imagine for a moment that I am unaware of the plastic bag containing marijuana pushed into the toe of the old tennis shoe you have stuffed at the back of your wardrobe.'

She was also unable to break herself of the habit of hitting me, even though I now hit her back. Our fights were desperate and hateful. Unable to bear punching her soft, weak, ageing body – afraid of doing her some permanent harm – I would grab her around the shoulders with both my arms and squeeze. Locked in this vicious mock-embrace we would wrestle, neither of us willing to submit – biting, scratching, pinching – crashing against the furniture until finally we stumbled and fell.

As if to prove that her parenting skills were no longer required, my mother began to make regular and extended pilgrimages to the United States. Ostensibly these visits were for the purpose of seeing my brother Nick, but in reality she spent much of the time with a lover, Jimmy. Shrewdly she kept her relationship with Jimmy – which had started before she became pregnant by my father and outlasted her marriage to him – concealed. After protesting for years at how deeply wounded she was by my father's infidelity she could scarcely admit to her own. My father, it subsequently emerged, knew everything, but – to his credit – said nothing. Even when my mother was berating him in front of me about his mistresses, he remained silent.

My father, incidentally, had been coming back to live at Brim Hill between his various affairs. It was always his policy to move in with his girlfriends, thus saving him the nuisance and expense of having to arrange accommodation of his own.

'If you take my advice, dear boy, you won't tie yourself down with property. You've no idea what a fag it is dealing with dry rot and plumbing and that sort of thing. Women are temperamentally more suited to it.'

Quite whom he lived with remains a mystery. I recall visiting him in a mansion block behind Harrods on one occasion, a mews house somewhere near Pimlico Underground station on another. He would often drop completely from view so that the only way to get in touch with him was to leave messages with the switchboard operator at the London School of Economics.

My father's unwillingness to find his own place meant that at the conclusion of each alliance he was rendered homeless. If no obvious alternative presented itself he would move into his club, which provided a number of spartan and inexpensive bedrooms for the use of its members. From the public telephone in the hallway he would mount an intensive campaign for reinstatement at Brim Hill.

'Ah, Johnny, everything all right? Good. Get your mother quickly, would you, I am in a call box.'

'What do you want, Peter? I am busy.'

'Bunchy, listen,' my father's booming voice so loud that I could listen, too, from the upstairs landing, 'have you any idea what it costs to rent a small flat? It is quite impossible on my income when I give you so much money. Sorry, but I am going to have to cut back on the alimony payments.'

'You can't,' my mother instantly hysterical, 'we are struggling already.'

'Well, there it is. The choice is yours.'

'Are you threatening me? Do you dare to threaten me?'

On and on until the change ran out, or my mother agreed – purely on grounds of economy – to let him sleep on the sofa. Once established there, providing he looked sufficiently contrite, it was only a matter of time before his return to the bedroom.

Soon after one such reconciliation my mother went off, as usual, to stay with Jimmy. When she came home my father had not only left her again, but had publicly announced his intention to marry Sandra Moiseiwitsch, the woman he had thrown over for Diana, his first wife. My mother was furious. Prior to her departure it had been agreed, supposedly once and for all, that she and my father would spend their old age together. I immediately resumed my role as her primary confidant. I had never seen her so angry or distraught. Violent and inconsolable, she railed against my father while I attempted unsuccessfully to calm and reassure her. I expect that she was really much crosser with herself than she was with him. Knowing that my father could not possibly have been expected to survive for six whole weeks without female company, she had still gone to America. If you wanted to hang on to my father it was fatal to leave him unattended.

Since my mother didn't raise any objections, I began to spend long periods away from home. Francesca and Freya

110

regularly took me in for weeks on end, but mostly I stayed with my girlfriend, June.

In an environment where furtive liaisons were the norm, perhaps it isn't particularly surprising that I entered into a clandestine relationship with a married woman. Ironically there was no question of deceiving June's husband, as they had an open marriage. Although he and I never discussed the subject, he was fully aware of how things stood between his wife and me. Indeed, he treated me as a member of their family – offering me support, advice and even financial assistance. Over time the two of us developed a lasting and quite separate, if somewhat unconventional, friendship of our own.

The reason why strict secrecy was observed lay in the fact that June was some thirty years my senior. As one would expect under the circumstances, there was a predictability to certain aspects of our relationship. June taught and I learned; she nurtured and I grew; sometimes, with the callous indifference of a teenager, I inadvertently hurt her. On the other hand, our relationship had a spiritual dimension. We met as true partners – giving, taking and sharing in equal measure. I loved June, and she loved me. Nevertheless, despite the strength and depth of our feelings for each other, we both understood the impossibility of our situation. For over five years – from when I was sixteen virtually until I met Jo, my first wife – we came together and parted, came together and parted, in a cycle of hope and despair.

June owned a large, rambling house set in several acres near the sea which, although located in the heart of a village, was concealed from view by a high flint wall. Hidden away in this safe, private haven, pretence was unnecessary, for among June's immediate circle our alliance was fully acknowledged and accepted. It was to here we retreated whenever we could manage it.

My mother was desperately jealous. She had no idea that June and I were a couple; she just hated being excluded. For the first time ever I had completely removed myself from her sphere of influence. I was doing things, meeting people, going places well beyond her ken.

'You're planning to be with them for the entire summer? I can't believe they really want you for such a long period. Especially as you were there for Easter as well. Not to mention all those weekends.'

Taking a leaf from her own book, I lied, exaggerating a genuine friendship with June's two youngest children (who were approximately my age) into something more.

'Well, it all seems very odd to me, Jonathan.'

Life with June contrasted sharply to life in Brim Hill. June was happy. Her husband and children were happy, too. It was a revelation to come into contact with a family who enjoyed themselves so much, took pleasure in one another's company. Of course, they had their ups and downs, but they tackled problems together; confided in and took comfort from each other. Never before had I encountered tolerance, understanding and consideration between such close relatives.

On my fortieth birthday June gave me back my letters, a thick, brown gusseted envelope stuffed with sheets of paper. I barely recognised the handwriting, let alone the words.

'I didn't want them to embarrass you after I die.'

I protested.

'Still,' she said, 'there they all are. You were prolific, weren't you? Though half the time you simply sent me diary entries. Why don't you read me something.'

I extracted a single, lined page at random and began to read to her – half recalling the events it described as I went.

'We didn't leave London until almost midnight. Wonderful drive. Just the two of us hurtling through the sleeping towns and villages. All too soon we were on the last lane to the village, winding down the windows so that we could breathe deep, cold, briny draughts of air. We had to search for the key in the woodshed, but finally discovered it. I think the click that the heavy latch on the back door makes will be a sound I remember all my life. Lights on. Sweet damp smell – the house not warm – the two of us shivering and laughing. Bags and baskets emptied from the car. A tray of tea and chocolate digestives.

'Three o'clock in the morning? Four o'clock in the morning? Far away church bells strike the hour, their pure notes carried to us on the chilly, night air. The ceiling seems to be the sky – hanging high and majestic above us – infinite. The windows are beaded with condensation, lit by the rays of the moon. Emptied of thought – sleep.

'Sunday papers from the shop. Tea and toast in bed. A walk on the beach – sea running high. No one about. You had various chores to perform and I watched some television. A delicious supper, an early night. What can I say – an absolutely perfect weekend. Tenderness. Contentment. We talked. We were silent. Up this morning at five so as not to get caught in traffic.'

All the homes I have ever owned have been an attempt to recreate the same relaxed, welcoming atmosphere as June's seaside house. It was very much her house, her husband rarely appeared, and she made its management appear effortless. Each day might bring new arrivals or departures, there were rarely less than ten of her family or friends in residence, yet she was never flustered and did not fuss about domestic arrangements. Instead, she appeared to have limitless amounts of time to spend with her children and guests. She rode; gardened; read the paper; pottered in the kitchen; organised treats. Despite all the comings and goings the household rolled along at a remarkably calm and relaxed pace. Breakfast was a self-service affair. Lunch was informal –

113

June would put out soup, bread, cheese, pâté without really knowing how many would attend or when. Indeed, the evening was the only occasion when everyone gathered together in one place. From about six o'clock onwards the kitchen would fill up as different members of the party began preparing different elements of the dinner, or came in to chat with those who were. At seven-thirty or eight the enormous table would be laid – possibly for as many as twenty – and the meal would be served. Around ten-thirty or quarter to eleven those with sufficient energy would rush down to the pub for a late night drink. The rest would gradually disappear, to bed or other pursuits, though as late as twelve or one in the morning there could still be half a dozen people sitting around and talking. The nicest thing about June's house was that it was always filled with the sound of cheerful voices and laughter.

June's family spent Christmas there and I usually joined them on Boxing Day (or as soon after as I could manage) to participate in the New Year festivities. The big event was a pantomime, written and acted out by the entire household, to which everyone in the village was invited. One year it snowed and the evening took on the enchanted quality of a scene from a Victorian novel. The audience were guided to the door by burning torches and warmed themselves in front of a roaring fire with hot punch and mince pies. We performed an improvised version of Cinderella (I was an ugly sister) and afterwards a late supper was served. Unlike Christmas with my mother – a strained business that invariably ended in a screaming match if not actual bloodshed – June's family celebrated the season with parties, games, tournaments, trips, riotous drinking sessions and lengthy, numbingly cold, but spectacular tramps along the beach. This, it seemed to me, was precisely what life should be like. My ambition, which hitherto had been focused solely on escape, began to widen. I realised that what I wanted, more than any-thing else, was to build my own version of this world.

The year I met June I left school and went away with my father.

We travelled as Professor and Mrs Self. My airline ticket even had 'Mrs Self' printed on it. Frequently our hosts, expecting a Mrs Self, having laid on hospitality for a Mrs Self, proved loath to alter their arrangements. Thus, in Hong Kong, while my father met the Governor, I was taken dress shopping by the Governor's wife. In Delhi we were booked into a honeymoon suite.

Finding himself unexpectedly without a Mrs Self only days before he was due to leave for a six-month sabbatical over-seas, my father had invited me to accompany him.

'Sandra can't take the time off work. Your mother is out of the question. Seems a shame to waste a free ticket.'

We made a leisurely progress towards Australia, visiting a sprinkling of former LSE students in their home countries as we passed.

'Ken has done well for himself,' my father said with consid-erable satisfaction, as we sat in the back of a chauffeur-driven limousine on the way to yet another dinner in his honour, 'he is Minister of Education here, you know.'

The shy young men with broken English I remembered from tea in East Finchley had become national leaders – politicians and civil servants. My father was fêted wherever we went, treated as a guest of state. I refused to be impressed. Inculcated by my mother to believe that my father was a failure, I assumed that those who praised him must also be of no account. Soon after we arrived in Canberra he came home and announced that the next day he was to meet the Prime Minister. I shrugged my shoulders and said I hoped he didn't expect me to iron him a shirt.

'I'll iron my own bally shirt.' From the way he spoke I knew that for once I had managed to wound him. Triumphant, I flounced out. An hour later I returned, guiltily, to see how he was getting on.

'Ah, there you are,' pride in his voice, 'I've not only done my shirts, but some of yours as well. See.'

Crumpled shirts were hung all over the dining room. My father stood, iron in hand, looking very pleased with himself. I resisted the urge to tell him he had wasted his time, that an iron only works if it is plugged in.

'Well done, Dad. That was extremely sweet of you.'

I was there in place of his wife and, in a curious way, that was the role I fulfilled. We lived in a flat on the university campus and I occupied myself doing domestic chores and joining the wives of the other visiting academics in their activities. I took on various temporary jobs. I nagged and complained, as my mother had taught me to do. My father was polite but distant. Boredom ate away at me. I longed to be back in England. It was the most time we ever spent in each other's company. Both of us were grateful when it was over.

Absolutely rolling in oof

Will was, to my certain knowledge, in the janitor's cupboard snogging Beryl Bainbridge.

I was in the stationery cupboard snogging Sarah Thomson.

Our mother, when last spotted, had been sprawled on a chair with her feet up on a window sill trying to adjust her false teeth. One of her shoes was missing.

It was December 1977 and the occasion was the Duckworth Publishing Christmas Party. I attended several of these affairs and all of them began decorously enough. The main office would be cleared (usually it was crammed with boxes of books, there being insufficient warehousing space) and decorated with paperchains and balloons. The staff shared the burden of catering and they would all bring in things they had made at home, setting the food out on desks and improvised tables. The quantity of drink ordered for this annual event can only be described as fantastic. The firm's proprietor, Colin Haycraft, spent the whole morning personally supervising its unloading and preparation. Then, at around midday, he would call his employees together and wish them a merry Christmas. This was followed by a glass of champagne and some polite milling around, during which colleagues who had spent the previous year locked in mortal combat would exchange brittle pleasantries and compliment one another on their guacamole dips. The first guests would arrive, embarrassed to have turned up so early. Bit by bit the enormous room would fill up, corks popping in rapid succession like automatic gunfire, the barmen straining to keep pace with the demand for alcohol, the gentle murmur of earnest, intellectual conversation gradually giving way to the incoherent roar of a drunken crowd.

As I remember the 1977 party, by five o'clock those foolish enough – or wise enough, depending on your perspective – to have made plans for the afternoon had long since taken their leave. Few of the remaining revellers were standing unaided. Some were shoring up the walls and bookcases; others sat slumped wherever they could find a horizontal surface; a third group were lying down. Private subsidiary parties were taking place in the darker and more secluded corners of the building.

In our dark and secluded corner Sarah and I were having trouble breathing. We had been introduced by my mother barely an hour previously and when, after chatting for a while, Sarah had suggested that we find a cupboard to call our own it had taken me a moment or two to grasp the full meaning of her proposal. I was flattered, because she was undeniably pretty, and now that we were in the cupboard I was loath to move – even though it was getting uncomfortably hot and stuffy.

'Listen, duckie,' Sarah finally whispered into my ear during a break in the proceedings, 'it's a bit of a squeeze in here. Why don't you come back to my flat for a drink and something to eat?'

'OK.'

'See if there is anyone outside.'

Cautiously I opened the door a crack. 'No.'

Hand in hand, we found our coats and sneaked away. I moved in with Sarah a few days later.

My mother was extremely proprietorial about Duckworth.

As the production assistant she held a relatively junior position, but nevertheless she was immersed – to the point of excess – in its politics. She complained of sleepless nights spent worrying about its management; and if things were not going well at work she could speak of nothing else. She was the oldest person in the organisation and made great play of her age, using it as an excuse to proffer advice and wisdom to everyone from the chairman down. As well as performing her own duties she attempted to interfere in all sorts of areas which were none of her business – such as the way Colin's secretary laid out his letters or the effectiveness of the sales team. For the most part I think the other members of staff looked upon my mother as being relatively innocuous and essentially a benign – if neurotic – force. However, she had managed to infuriate one or two of them, and as a result was engaged in several long-running and bitter feuds. My mother was deadly earnest about these feuds and she was always keen to enlist additional support for her cause. This was one of the reasons why I think she was so enthusiastic about my romance with Sarah, who, as Duckworth's financial director, had the potential to be a powerful and well-placed ally. Intriguingly, no mention was ever made of the fact that Sarah was thirty-three while I was still only eighteen – which makes me wonder if my mother might not, after all, have accepted my relationship with June as being perfectly normal.

Immediately after I went to live with Sarah my mother put Brim Hill up for sale, saying: 'The risk is too great. While I have three bedrooms there is always the chance you might come back.' She wasn't being unkind. We all hated that house, the repository of so much despair, and my departure gave her the excuse she needed to be shot of it. Free of my father, free of me, free of Brim Hill – and with Will virtually off her hands – my mother became a considerably happier woman. Her new flat in Kentish Town was small, but as she never ceased to inform anyone who would listen, 'I love my flat. Absolutely love my flat. I love it.'

For my mother, part of its charm was due to the occupants of the other flats in the building. 'There's James on the top floor.' Naturally, she knew everything about her immediate neighbours within hours of her arrival. 'Gay, but a sweetie. It would kill his father if he found out, which means you must promise never to tell a soul. Right above me is a lovely girl, Catherine. Why she doesn't have a boyfriend I can't understand. Downstairs is Marcel, a terribly distinguished journalist. He says he can only write when there is lots of noise because he is used to a newsroom, which is why he doesn't mind me stamping around, bless him. We've agreed to have regular house dinners. Perhaps every fortnight. Catherine and I are going to the theatre on Thursday.'

She stuffed the flat with furniture, knick-knacks and, of course, her beloved books. Within such a confined and over-crowded space, members of the Self family – being tall, bulky and poorly coordinated – found that movement posed certain logistical problems. Our progress from room to room was invariably marked by exclamations and expletives as we sent first one thing and then another flying. Lack of space did not, however, stop my mother from entertaining. By opening the connecting door between the living room and the bedroom (Will slept in a sort of blocked-off corridor) she could seat twelve for dinner and there was a sofa bed for anyone who wanted to stay.

My mother also became gripped by a desire to travel. Initially, she took modest enough trips with women friends. 'Sheila and I are spending next week on Lundy'; 'I am showing Nina Walberswick and then we will be touring Constable country.'

But in time she became more adventurous. 'I have taken a house in Alicante for the winter'; 'I may be overweight and over the hill, but not so overweight and over the hill that I can't try my hand at skiing.'

News from abroad was relayed – sometimes daily – by postcard. 'Dank, gloomy apartment in the old town. Snap, snap, snap go the traps. Meep, meep, meep go the mice. Can't sleep for the sound of dying Spanish rodents. Read Flaubert all day in a sidewalk café.' These brief, scribbled missives furnished a vivid picture of her life. 'Last night I forced two new acquaintances – Sebastian and Carlos – to share a double bed (although there are plenty of single rooms in the villa), believing them to be embarrassed about their homosexual relationship. Wouldn't listen to their protests. Explained how broad-minded I was. Horror of horrors. Discovered this morning that they really are just friends – both happily married with children.'

Away for months on end, her communications frequently took on a slightly surreal quality: 'Would you object to me marrying a Tuscan butcher who doesn't speak a word of English Question mark Love Mummy,' queried a telegram.

Jimmy dumped her. She never told me how long they had been together, or what he had meant to her, just that it was over. The subsequent railing and wailing lacked conviction, barely anything hurled about or smashed, leaving me with the impression that Jimmy's defection was not entirely unwelcome.

She never entirely lost her interest in men, but following the break up with Jimmy she ceased to be dependent on them.

'Leon makes an excellent travel companion,' she said of a possible suitor, 'but I wouldn't want to live with him.'

My mother's sixtieth birthday found her in rude health and excellent spirits.

'I had been hoping', she told party guests, 'that the bus conductor would accuse me of lying when I produced my free pass. "Surely not you, madam?" I expected him to cry out in surprise.'

She bought herself a new bike and we went through a brief phase of cycling around London with one another. To Columbia Road market to buy plants for her garden, to Regent's Park for morning coffee, to the Serpentine Gallery to see an exhibition. Our relationship, which had been improving since the day I left home, now became much more of a friendship. I withheld information about myself which I knew instinctively would lead to disapproval or conflict – June remained a secret – but in general was much more open with her. Sarah was replaced by Lorraine, and Lorraine by Philippa, and Philippa by Mary-Anne, and my mother met them all. Indeed, she fussed over my girlfriends as if they were her own daughters. She invited them to her flat without me, took them shopping, gave them presents, donated her old clothes to them, and even wrote to my father about them.

'Mum tells me you have left home and moved in with someone called Sarah.'

'Actually, we broke up, Dad.'

'Oh. Hope you aren't too upset.'

'No. it's fine. I'm living at Francesca's in Fellows Road.'

There was a pause while my father chewed thoughtfully on his steak.

'I hope she isn't charging you rent.'

Any conversation with my father during this period tended to work itself around to the same topic: money, and his impending financial crisis. The London School of Economics was forcing him to retire with the result that his income would be insufficient to support his various dependants.

'There's your mother, your stepmother, your younger brother, your stepsister, your grandmother.' It was my father's practice to use and stress the possessive adjective when describing mutual relatives: your, your, your, your. A forlorn attempt to shift responsibility away from himself.

'Then there are pensions for Doris, your grandmother's cook; Elsie, your grandfather's secretary; and Murphy,' he sighed ruefully and shook his head, apparently oblivious to the semi-clad waitress topping up his wine. He had telephoned me at work that afternoon to say he was in London and felt a bit low. To cheer him up I was treating him to dinner at the Playboy Club. 'I also try to send a little money to Alison and Mrs Mac.'

He brightened. 'Still, dear boy, you are doing well and that is a relief.' He smiled and allowed his gaze to wander around the restaurant. 'Must be expensive here.'

'Not really, Dad, the food is subsidised by the gambling. I'll take you up to the gaming rooms later.'

'The thing is,' he suddenly looked sheepish, 'I've been offered a permanent job in Australia. Sandra wants to go. It would be extremely well paid. What do you think?'

I could tell he had already decided. My father was like that. Minor decisions were discussed ad nauseam, the major ones presented fait accompli. I was touched, though, that he had bothered to consult me.

'If it is what you want, Dad. Have you considered Granny? She is nearly ninety.'

'Yes, Granny will miss me.'

Granny did miss him. My mother was euphoric; Will and I were indifferent; his other family members and friends oddly ambivalent; but my grandmother felt his absence keenly and never gave up hope that he might return.

'Does your father say anything when he writes to you?' she would ask plaintively, her eyes filling with tears. 'I do wish he would at least consider coming back. He can be quite exasperating.'

'I'm afraid he hasn't mentioned coming back, except for a

visit, Granny.' His letters for the next two decades were awash with possible travel arrangements. He and Sandra might spend Christmas in England. He might make the journey alone in the spring. She might come first in May and he might join her in July. They would route themselves via Canada, Hong Kong, Austria. Their stay would be a month, two months, three months. The economy fare with one airline had gone up, the business fare with a different airline could be about to fall. We learned not to expect him until we saw him.

My father didn't write often, perhaps every couple of months, but when he did he wrote at length. Half of his letters were devoted to his own news, half to answering whatever points I had made in my previous letter to him. His literary style was eccentric, peppered freely with old-fashioned expressions. 'Have you', he once enquired, 'formed any new romantic attachments?' The first house I purchased was referred to as 'your charming artisan's dwelling'. He was also something of an emotional bureaucrat and liked feelings to be neat and tidy. 'Either you are keen on her or you aren't,' he insisted when I appeared to be vacillating about a prospective girlfriend.

The advice he offered, and there was no shortage of it, tended to be both clichéd and confused. 'I don't agree with Mum about the immorality of a good income provided it is well earned. But I do believe in not counting your chickens before hatched and keeping your feet on the ground – so don't throw too many balls in the air. I can imagine well how laborious it is for you to steer a patient and steady course under the present circs with a real eye to the future.'

He had a tendency, too, to jump from subject to subject without warning. 'Sydney still seems very prosperous, lovely seafood restaurants, but we are cutting down alas on rich foods. Mrs T is becoming more impossible over the unions

126

not to mention over the EEC – a thorny problem – I believe national states may be on the way out, despite a lot of jingoism knocking around. You never said much about your trip to New York.'

He fancied himself as something of a photographer and took hundreds of shots a year using an ancient, one-setting Instamatic purchased in the early 1970s for which (to his disgust) it had become increasingly difficult to find film. Every envelope that arrived bulged with captioned 'snaps': 'An intriguing lady on a ferry. No idea who she is'; 'You can't see it, but there is a koala at the top of this tree'; 'Ticket kiosk at Jervis Bay National Park. Sandra in background'; 'Car park of my office building in Canberra.'

Over-exposed and out of focus, they presented a peculiarly bright and blurry vision of his life in Australia – perpetual sunshine, everything slightly rushed. The country had certainly infused him with hitherto unimaginable levels of energy. He was lecturing at the university; publishing books and articles; acting as a government adviser. Sandra had persuaded him to perform voluntary work in the local hospice. On top of which came golf, bush-walking, gardening and the usual socialising. Indeed, his social life alone beggared belief.

'Out every night this week,' he regularly reported, 'bridge Monday at Angela's, theatre Tuesday, the Parkers' for dinner Wednesday, a church barbecue Thursday and Pat's book launch Friday. Saturday Roger and Anne have invited us to a party.' It was a pattern of activity he maintained throughout his sixties and seventies.

His marriage was stormy. He considered Sandra to be intellectually inferior, and even boasted about it. 'My mistake with Diana and your mother was to marry intelligent women. Unlike Sandra, they weren't satisfied to be housewives.'

Sandra berated him continuously, however, for many of the same things which had irritated my mother. In an unusually introspective mood he remarked: 'I've arranged for Sandra to make my bed, I suppose I must lie in it.'

Nevertheless, for all the rowing there was no doubting my father's devotion to Sandra, her daughter Karin and grand-daughter Anna. 'I am treating the three girls to a holiday on the Barrier Reef'; 'Karin is short of cash and, naturally, I am going to stump up'; 'Anna is coming out to live with us for a year.'

I harboured the suspicion that this new family was more important to him than the one he had left behind.

'Should I come back, I wonder?'

I had telephoned to let him know that his mother was seriously ill.

'Hard to say, Dad. On the whole I think you should.'

'Perhaps I'll leave it for a few days and see if she rallies.'

In all the years he lived in Australia no medical emergency was ever deemed sufficiently grave to bring him rushing back to England. His mother, his ex-wife, his brother, several of his best friends, his step-granddaughter Anna – all died while he waited to see if they might rally. Yet ironically, on paper at least, he showed a much greater sensitivity. His letters oozed encouragement, sympathy and regret. From twelve thousand miles away he expressed more pride in my achievements, a deeper concern over my disappointments, than he seemed able to manage at closer range.

Birthdays and Christmases were marked with cards and presents. Books on subjects in which I had no interest, posted at enormous expense, bore sad little inscriptions: 'To Dearest Johnny. Thinking of you and missing you. Love Dad.'

Confronted with my reality he appeared to miss me less. On his trips back to England I was one of perhaps thirty or forty people to be fitted into his schedule, and by no means top of the list. He wasn't exactly unenthusiastic about spending time with me, but he certainly didn't cancel anything else for the privilege. If his visit was short, we would meet for dinner at the Reform Club – frequently with Will, Karin and others so that he could cross several of us off at once. If he was around for longer, or if he was in need of accommodation, he might invite himself for a stay.

Though I found fault with everything my father said and did, sneered at his sentimentality, he was capable of surprising me.

'It goes without saying, darling, that I would be pleased to assist. How much do you need?'

It was the only occasion in my adult life that I had asked him for money.

'I am afraid it is rather a lot, Dad. Fifteen thousand.'

'Fifteen thousand?' He looked incredulous but then, seeing I was in earnest, became thoughtful.

My father wasn't naturally generous and had the infuriating habit of retrospectively attaching conditions to any act of kindness. 'You know that antique table I gave you?' One of several items he had not wanted to ship to Australia. 'I thought that in exchange you might treat Sandra and me to our forthcoming holiday.'

He always felt justified in allowing anyone he perceived to be richer than himself to pick up the tab. 'Maurice is incredibly wealthy. Let him fork out for the party.'

In his eyes I was 'absolutely rolling in oof' and as a result he felt no compunction in allowing me to pay whenever the chance arose. I didn't mind. It allowed me to show off. Will always thought that he was envious of our financial success. I rather suspect that our father's overriding emotion was one of hopelessness. His children were independent and headstrong. We didn't need him for anything. He was redundant. When it looked as if I might be going bankrupt, he told Will: 'There is no point in handing your brother a single penny. He is in such trouble that nothing I could spare would make any difference.'

At the time I assumed he was being parsimonious and had resented it. Now I wonder if it wasn't spoken with regret on his part. How could he help a son who was so self-reliant? After all, when I did ask for help his response was unequivocal.

'Fifteen thousand, Johnny?'

'Listen, don't worry Dad. I'm sorry I asked.'

'No. I can definitely help if you can wait a couple of weeks.'

He'll drink neat vodka, or ruddy nothing

I was woken from a dreamless sleep by a loud cracking sound.
I lay in the pitch black feeling queasy and confused. There it
was again. I listened carefully. Someone was outside the
window attempting to break in. Alarmed, I sat on the edge of
the bed and began to search the floor for a weapon with
which to defend myself. As my hand closed around a shoe the
casement shot up and a gust of wind blew the curtains back.
I leapt to my feet, ready to strike.

'Will?'

'What?'

'Will, is that you?'

'No. It is his brother, Jonathan.'

'Sorry, I thought it would be Will.'

Before I could reply a figure dressed in a silver jumpsuit
clambered through the window. Hastily I dropped the shoe
and pulled on some underwear.

'How do you do? I'm Will Sieghart.'

'How do you do?'

More clambering.

'This is Ben. Ben, this is Will's brother, Jonathan.'

'Hello.'

'Hello.'

'Will's usually still up at this hour,' said a cross voice from
outside the window.

'He's with Penny,' I explained.

'Oh.'

Three or four additional bodies scrambled through and crowded into the room. In the dark it was hard to see exactly what was happening.

'Only way to get in once the porters have closed the college gates. Sorry to have disturbed you.'

'Don't mention it.'

The group began to file out through the door. As Will Sieghart was leaving he hesitated for a moment.

'I say, I don't suppose Will left any of his dope here?'

'No, we smoked it all.'

I visited Will most weekends during his fresher year at Oxford. Generously he gave me his room in Exeter College, moving over the road to stay with his longstanding girlfriend – Penny Phillips – in Balliol. It was a period of rediscovery for us. After I had left home we saw very little of each other. I can't remember him ever coming to any of the places where I lived or to Walberswick and, of course, we had both grown up keeping the greater part of our lives secret from one another. Our childhood experiences had isolated us – in some respects we were more like strangers than brothers. We didn't discuss our emotions. We made barely any reference to our parents or to our shared past. There was always a degree of antagonism between us, too. Yet simultaneously there was an exceptionally strong fraternal bond. We were intensely loyal. We struggled to be closer. Deep down I was aware of his suffering, he of mine, and it united us. Crucially, we enjoyed the same sense of humour. No subject was ever so sacred that we didn't try to get a laugh out of it. This is a verbatim account of the somewhat disrespectful telephone conversation we had when my father's brother unexpectedly died.

'Bad news. Uncle Mike dropped dead addressing an envelope. He was sending off a cheque to pay the rates.'

'You are joking.'

'No. Dad just rang. Apparently Aunt Penny went into the kitchen to fetch a banana and when she came back a minute later he was dead.'

'If it had been a different fruit perhaps he'd still be alive.'

'No wife of mine goes into the kitchen for a banana when I'm addressing envelopes.'

'Shame she didn't pick a safer fruit. Cherries or grapes. Bananas are obviously lethal.'

'It's the combination. Bananas and addressing an envelope. Probably wouldn't have happened if he had paid the rates by direct debit. Foolish man.'

'Really. Did I mention Justin's uncle died reading in bed.'

'My God, I had no idea that that could be such a dangerous pastime. Perhaps it was his choice of literature. Any idea what he was reading?'

At eighteen Will already exerted the most extraordinary hold over people. He was surrounded by acolytes. They hung about his room drinking, taking drugs and listening to him expound. It was a stimulating if occasionally dangerous environment. For, although Will's conversation sparkled, he could turn nasty, and even his most devoted disciples were not exempt from censure.

'Geoff, that was a stupid thing you just said.'

Weakly, Geoff tried to counter the attack. 'It wasn't. And if it was, haven't you ever said anything stupid yourself, Will?'

'Nothing as stupid as what you just said, Geoff. Give me that flannel someone, it'll have to do.' Will put the flannel on his head. 'Now, Geoff, I will pass sentence. For expressing that particularly ill-informed and ignorant thought regarding existentialism, you will be taken from this place to another place where, without the aid of lubricant, a copy of Jean-Paul Sartre's complete works will be inserted in your anus – it clearly being the orifice out of which you speak – in the hope its contents will permeate your consciousness and thus prevent you from expressing so dullwitted a sentiment ever again.'

It was during a weekend partying in Oxford that I was introduced to Jo. Nat was conceived within days of our initial date. Jo had grown up with Will's best friend at university, Ben. By trade she was a croupier. A tall, striking girl, she had started out in the Playboy Club where she went by the name of Bunny Coral until she scratched off the letter 'C' for a joke and was fired by the Bunny Mother.

When Jo was young, maybe twelve, her parents decided after supper one evening that they would emigrate to Australia – literally – the following day. They took their dog, but left behind their daughter. She came home from school and found the house locked up, so being a sensible girl she moved into the vacated kennel (which was apparently quite spacious) until rescued by Ben's mother, Mo, who was the local schoolteacher. I heard this story from Mo, so I am inclined to believe it. In a way it was probably something of a blessing for Jo. Her father had spent all of the previous year in their attic, relieving himself through a large plastic pipe which ran down through a hole he had drilled in the bathroom ceiling and ended up in the wc. That was the same year her mother began to hear voices at night and came to believe that she could speak in tongues. These two facts about her parents would alone appear to justify almost any degree of eccentricity in Jo.

The decision to get pregnant was very much Jo's and taken without consulting me. The decision to have a 'hoover job', as she referred to an abortion, was also hers, and again my opinion was not sought. When she changed her mind a third time she simply said: 'You know I wasn't supposed to eat anything for twelve hours before this afternoon's hoover job? Well, I got hungry this morning and had a massive breakfast of ham and eggs.'

Leaving me to work out the implications. 'You mean you are going to have the baby?'

'Yes. And if you aren't kind to me, my older brother will come and beat you up.'

The threat was unnecessary: I was thrilled at the idea of becoming a father. I was besotted with Jo and told her how much I loved her several times a day. She was honest enough never to reply in the same vein. I was foolish enough not to notice.

Far from being dismayed by the fact her middle son was to become a father at twenty-two, my mother exulted in it. Here was an event, a cause, which could readily be turned into high emotional drama. Jo and I were summoned repeatedly to Kentish Town where food and advice were forced upon us in equal measure. During one of these visits, while Jo was out of the room, my mother lowered her voice and said: 'You had better get married to her.'

It wasn't a question, or a statement, but a command. I bridled. But I bridled in a whisper. 'Why?' I hissed back.

'Just trust me. Get married.'

'But, why?'

'Since you ask, I'll tell you. If you aren't married to the mother of your child, you have no rights – no rights what-soever – as a father.'

'How do you know?'

'I read it in the *Guardian*. Jo can force you to pay for the child's upbringing. But you can't force her to give you access. You must marry her.'

I doubted, even as she spoke, that my mother had got this entirely right. I recognised, too, that her sympathies lay wholly with Jo, who was, after all, doing to me virtually what my mother had done to my father. Yet so dominant was her influence that on the strength of this hasty conversation I proposed to Jo as soon as we were alone.

Jo and I had trouble taking her pregnancy seriously. We enrolled for natural childbirth classes but, due to our undisguised mirth at the sight of half a dozen Clapham couples on their hands and knees panting as if their lives depended on it, we were asked not to attend a second time. We got the wrong day for the antenatal surgery and couldn't be bothered to rebook.

'When I go into labour,' pointed out Jo, 'those doctors and midwives are bound to know what to do. Stands to reason. Why should we worry?'

She spent a very pleasant afternoon cutting out material with which to make baby clothes. Her interest in this project waned, however, long before the sewing stage. We passed a glorious hour composing a list of all the things we meant to borrow or buy for baby, and then immediately lost it. Some rash late night let's-redecorate-prior-to-the-big-day talk prompted me to rush out early one morning and purchase a blow torch, with which I set fire to the bannisters while attempting to strip paint, before Jo confiscated it. In the end we confined ourselves to emptying a drawer for baby's bed, and converting the vegetable basket into a bassinet. Our sole meaningful concession to the forthcoming arrival was to renounce tobacco, marijuana and alcohol.

There has been a certain amount of competition between my brother Will and me about our respective drink problems. He believes I exaggerate:

'I don't know why you persist in thinking you are an alcoholic.'

'Volume. Effect. Desire.'

'Yes, but you were hardly drinking lighter fluid under Charing Cross Bridge at fifteen.' Spoken scathingly, with the tone of a man who might well have been himself. Not that he was.

I started drinking heavily while I was still at school. An overpowering urge to get completely drunk on a frequent basis was combined with a high level of tolerance. As the years passed I began to suspect I might have a problem and imposed an ever-changing variety of drinking rules on myself – nothing until after dinner, for instance, or nothing before lunch, or no spirits during the week – all of which I broke with a predictable regularity. It got to the stage where if I didn't have a drink in front of me, I was thinking about when I would, and if I did, I was thinking about the next drink. In order not to drink alone I drank with people whose company I didn't enjoy. Most tellingly of all, I kept my true levels of alcohol consumption to myself. I learned how to sneak in extra drinks when no one was looking. Prior to meeting Jo, I had started to have blackouts.

I was surprised at how effortlessly I was able give it all up. I vaguely recall feeling as if I had a dreadful dose of the flu, being in a foul humour for several days, then forgetting about the whole thing.

I had developed a pretty ferocious temper by the time I was twenty-one. My mood swings were mercurial and astonished me every bit as much as they did anyone who happened to witness them. Calm and imperturbable one moment, a ridiculously insignificant event would send me berserk the next. When the television remote control didn't work I jumped up and down on it until it was in fragments. When I caught a neighbour's cat in our kitchen I flung an open bottle of milk at it. When the water heater finally gave up the ghost I ripped the whole device off the wall. There was a tension to being around me which even I found difficult to bear. Jo undoubtedly suffered the worst of it.

'What the fuck do you mean, you forgot to collect my dry-cleaning? How many fucking times did I mention it to you? Look, here's the note I stuck to the kitchen table to remind you. I notice you managed to spend the whole fucking twenty pounds I left.'

Not that Jo wasn't capable of similar conduct herself. Furious with me for staying in the bath for too long she once threw every single item of my clothing – including the socks – out of our front window. It was a cold, wet, windy day and as – wearing only a towel – I attempted to retrieve those clothes which had not blown away, she locked me out.

I can access the powerful emotions I experienced when each of my boys was born with incredible ease: the wonder, joy and fulfilment of becoming a father. It brings tears to my eyes, a lump to my throat, just to think of the first time I clasped them in my arms. Nat arrived at eight minutes after eleven in the evening (I recall glancing at the clock and noting with the faintest pang of regret that the pubs were about to close), a serene, chubby thing with a full head of hair and sleepy blue eyes. I was so proud I telephoned my father straight away – from a call box in the hospital – though it was by no means easy since, by then, he had emigrated to Australia with Sandra.

'Hello, Dad?'

'Who is this?'

'Dad, it's me, Jonathan.'

'Who? Hang on a second. Is that Johnny?'

'Yes. Dad, I am a dad, too.'

'What time is it? It must be the middle of the night.'

'Late. I'm a dad, Dad.'

'What did you say?'

'Dad, I'm a father. You're a grandfather.'

'Has Jo had the baby?'

'Yes.'

'Well done, dear. Congratulations.'

'Thank you.'

'I expect you're tired.'

'Not in the least. It was a boy.'

'A boy? Excellent. Well, I mustn't keep you, this call will be costing you a bomb.'

According to my mother's version of events, when she went into labour with me my father dropped her off at Charing Cross Hospital and proceeded to Twickenham to watch a rugby match. Although I accept she was not the most reliable of witnesses, the story has more than a ring of plausibility to it. Naturally, I was determined to be different.

'Dad, I was there for the whole thing. It was incredible. You have no idea.'

'My dear fellow, how enterprising of you.'

I was suffused with love. Wanted nothing more than the pleasure of holding Nat, protecting him, caring for him. I walked around in a glow for weeks afterwards, blissfully content, bursting with energy, overflowing with optimism.

What optimism. At twenty-two I was without doubt, without fear. Looking after a baby seemed easy. With uncharacteristic patience I undertook my half of the feeding and bathing, changing and playing. It was an honour to get up in the night for Nat. A privilege to nurse him. He was such a placid, happy baby. Jo and I took him with us everywhere. To my office. To visit friends. To old haunts such as the Colony Rooms where the regulars fussed over him.

'What will your bleeding nipper have, then, Jo?'

'Orange juice and warm water in this bottle.'

'Orange juice and water? No soft drinks served in here, even to sprogs. He'll drink neat vodka or ruddy nothing.'

'Yes, give him a drop of vodka.'

'Never too soon for a taste of vodka.'

To our wedding at Putney Town Hall. An event which ended abruptly when the photographer made the mistake of asking the four proud parents-in-law to come together for a shot. My mother, who had been close to boiling point throughout the proceedings, erupted. 'If you think I am having my photograph taken with that fucking bastard, think again.'

In the silence which descended over our party my father was heard to answer: 'Can't you bloody pipe down for once? Let it go.'

As if this were the signal they had been waiting for, Jo's parents immediately launched into a separate, equally vitriolic spat. The wedding breakfast was a chilly business.

Now that we had a child, Jo's flat was no longer large enough. In 1983, a year after the riots, property in Brixton had plummeted in value. We found a late Georgian house close to the front line with all its original fireplaces and shutters and a long, narrow garden. Approached through the private lane at the back, which was lined with apple and pear trees, you could almost imagine that you were in the country. It had the added advantage of being opposite Brockwell Park.

A mild spring turned into a scorching summer. Nat woke at dawn and so did I. Leaving him in his pyjamas, I took him straight to the Brockwell Lido for a shower. I revelled in this daily ritual. With Nat perched precariously on my shoulders, my arms full of clean clothes and nappies, we would stroll through the park and steal through a side door left open as a courtesy to early morning swimmers. I loved being up and about before the rest of the world was stirring, when the loudest sound in the city was birdsong, and the air was fragrant with the sweet smell of freshly mown grass. We would sit and watch the deserted pool for a few moments – its icy-cold water dancing and sparkling in the sunlight – before performing our ablutions. It was a slow process getting Nat washed and dressed. Suddenly conscious that the day was slipping away, I would hoist Nat back up on to my shoulders and make a quick dash for home. With considerable reluctance he would be persuaded to eat a little breakfast, I'd clean him up, we'd play for a while (I could never bear to leave him), and then I'd pop him into bed with his mother before setting off for work. Usually they were back in bed when I came home.

'Jesus, Jo, when did you last change Nat's nappy?'

'I don't know. After lunch.'

'That's five hours ago. Honestly, the poor boy.'

'It won't kill him. I was busy.'

'He's filthy. There's mud all over the sheets. What has he been doing?'

'Playing in the garden. I was painting. He's probably been eating dirt again.'

'For fuck's sake, Jo, you've got to pay more attention to him.'

'Yeah, yeah, yeah. Did you bring home any food? I'm famished.'

'Yes. I'll make supper when I've dealt with Nat. Honestly. You really piss me off.'

'Yeah, yeah, yeah.'

My mother was enthralled with the idea of Nat, though she found the actuality of caring for him less appealing. Providing she didn't have sole custody, however, she was enthusiastic to play the part of the doting grandmother. The instant we arrived at her door she would snatch him away.

'Mummy and Daddy are cruel and horrid. Come to Greri.' Greri was the name she liked her grandchildren to call her by. She had invented it.

'I'm taking Nat to see the flowers on my balcony. Help yourselves to a drink, blighted parents.'

Within minutes she would be back.

'Why don't you hold him while I finish lunch?'

After which she would confine herself to theory as opposed to practice.

'You must stop breast-feeding. It is bad for him'; 'By

141

picking him up when he cries you are making a rod for your own back'; 'I'd rather he didn't do that.'

There was a cosiness to my mother's new domestic life – a sense of security and stability – that Jo and I found attractive. It was pleasant to sit around while she chatted and cooked. Jo drew, I read the newspaper, Nat crawled about pulling things over. My mother's friends came and went, meals were served, excursions taken. If the enjoyment of her hospitality meant enduring a moderate amount of criticism and occasional outbursts of anger (she could not shake off the tantrum habit), it was a small price to pay.

Blooded, as it were, by an unplanned child and all that followed, the bonds between my mother and me grew stronger. There were particular types of problem – primarily work related – over which I unfailingly consulted her. Above her fireplace she had stuck a poster featuring an illustration by William Morris and a quote from Sir Walter Scott: 'O what a tangled web we weave, when first we practise to deceive!' For advice regarding the manipulation of people or events she was without peer. In personal matters, however, I avoided her counsel. I did not admit to her, for instance, what a disaster my marriage was until after it was over.

What is this stuff again?

'Hurry up.'

While I was fumbling to get the front door open, Screech Girl pressed herself against me impatiently.

'You are so-o-o-o slow,' she whispered into my ear. Then she screeched with laughter. Whenever Screech Girl uttered something she considered to be amusing – and she believed pretty much everything she said could be classified thus – she screeched with laughter. The door finally yielded and in we fell, clutching at each other to prevent ourselves from tripping over. We kissed. She pulled away.

'Where's the loo?'

'Upstairs.'

I fetched a bottle of wine and some glasses.

'Mind if I look around?' She called over the bannisters. Screech.

'Be my guest.'

I heard her opening doors and switching on lights. She came downstairs slowly.

'You have children?'

'A boy.'

'You didn't mention that when you were chatting me up at the party.'

She wasn't screeching now.

'Didn't I?'

'Where is he?'

143

'He's with his mother.'

'You're married.'

'I'm not. My wife and I are separated. This is my house. She has never lived here.'

'Oh, yes,' she said, picking up her handbag, 'and the other one has bells on. Find a different sucker.'

After Screech Girl had gone I sat on the floor of Nat's room and put away his toys. There was a different coloured plastic crate for each category. Wooden train set in red. Duplo in blue. Cars in orange. Action Man in purple. Miscellaneous bits and pieces – string, figures, a broken alarm clock, masks, balls – in yellow. Books on his shelves. Art materials on his desk. Cuddly animals on his bed. There were enough toys to keep an army of small children occupied for weeks. When I had finished organising the toy boxes I took out a pile of his laundered T-shirts and buried my nose in them. I thought I could just detect the faintest whiff of my son. I got undressed, slid under his duvet, hugged a giant stuffed whale, and fell asleep.

Inexplicably, it always commenced in Whetstone High Road. When I was quite young my father used to drive us through Whetstone on the way to a favourite walk of his in Hadley Wood. Even as a child the place depressed me – an impenetrable jungle of brick villas – desolate, dreary and uninviting. To my mind Brim Hill was on the edge of civilisation and I viewed the suburbs further north as a wasteland fraught with danger.

During the first few seconds, aware of what was in store for me, I would struggle.

'For Christ's sake,' I would shout at myself, 'wake up.'

I knew subconsciously what to expect next and watched the horizon in anticipation. There it was. A dazzling flash of green light. Slowly a giant mushroom cloud formed in the sky above me. My heart stopped beating, my whole body became immobilised, as I tried to remember why the nuking of High Barnet was a more serious matter than it at first appeared. It came to me. Nat. What about Nat? He was in Brixton. I imagined him alone in the house, terrified, whimpering with fear. All I could think about was rushing to his side. I started to jog southwards.

In Temple Fortune I turned a corner and ran into a seething crowd of people with blood dribbling down their faces. They blocked my path but I forced myself through. In Golders Green several buildings had collapsed across the road but I was able to climb over the rubble and keep going. In Swiss Cottage I had to dodge a lunatic with a machine-gun who was spraying the Finchley Road with bullets. In St James's I found myself trapped in an enclosed space filled with deadly gases. In Victoria a swarm of bees attacked me. By some miracle I overcame each obstacle, only to see it replaced by another. North Lambeth was flooded. Kennington was in flames. Getting closer to Brixton, I could hear Nat's stifled screams of anguish. I was in despair of saving him.

I always woke up before I was able to reach him.

The dream began the night Jo left me, taking Nat with her, and it recurred with only minimal variation for months. It reflected, with absolute accuracy, how I felt, for the absence of physical daily contact with Nat robbed me of all rational thought. Anything and everything reminded me of my loss. A commercial for Nat's favourite breakfast cereal could reduce me to tears, a news story about something bad happening to a child might send me to bed for an afternoon. I was barely able to hold a normal conversation and my concentration was so badly affected that some days it took me hours to perform the most basic of tasks. Wherever I was, whatever I did, it felt wrong and as a consequence I changed many of my plans mid-course. I lost count of the number of times I bolted from restaurants before the food had been served or rushed from a Tube train before my destination had been reached. In one classic incident I flew to Scotland for a long weekend with my friend Kate, but came straight back because seeing her baby boy, Alexander, made me feel so insecure.

'I knew it. I knew it.' My mother wrung her hands in anguish. 'I knew Jo would leave you.'

It was still early, not yet nine o'clock, but she was ready for bed, caught out by my unexpected arrival.

'I knew it. I had a foreboding. I warned you.'

If she had, I couldn't recall it. Then again, she issued so many warnings it was hard to keep track.

'Where is Jo?'

'I have no idea. Not in London. She insists,' I hesitated and then blurted out the thing which was really upsetting me, 'she insists I won't see Nat again until I agree to move out of the house.'

A long silence. Embarrassed, I felt I should say something. 'She's run out of money and had to sell all her jewellery to live.'

This touched a nerve. 'Her jewellery? What the hell are you talking about?'

'I'm talking about Jo's jewellery.' Suddenly I am five, not twenty-five. 'She has sold it.'

'The only jewellery Jo had was the jewellery I gave her. My mother's jewellery. How could you be so stupid as to let her sell it?'

Protests that it wasn't my fault fell on deaf ears.

'How could you? How could she? This is a disaster.' She spoke with such vehemence that even today the loss of my son, my wife and my home remain inextricably linked in my mind with the loss of Grandma Lily's jewellery.

Next time Jo telephoned I ignored my solicitor's advice and agreed to move out. Three days without Nat had left me bereft.

If my father had taught me one thing, it was where to go when you break up with someone.

'Young Mr Self. Your first visit with us, isn't it? Doubtless, you've left your wife, sir?' enquired the Reform Club's lugubrious chamberlain, not entirely joking, as he served me tea the morning after my arrival.

'There isn't really room for you to stay here,' explained my mother when, later the same day, I telephoned looking for temporary accommodation. She was still furious with me over the jewellery. Despondent, I languished in the club for the following week, too depressed to go outdoors, let alone start searching for a flat. Hearing of my fate, Diana, my father's first wife, came to the rescue – insisting that I share her house for as long as I wanted. Her compassion and patience did much to alleviate the misery I felt after my separation from Jo. It was Diana with whom I now discussed concerns about Nat, my career, the forthcoming divorce; Diana who helped me find a new home in King's Cross and then lent me the cash with which to buy it.

Anguish at being without Nat was marginally offset by relief at being released from my marriage to Jo. I was furious with her for stealing our son, but strangely grateful to her for having had the courage to terminate our relationship, all the more so as she did it in such a manner as to exonerate me from any sense of guilt. She achieved this through the simple enough expedient of having an affair and then running off with her lover. With typical self-delusion I convinced myself that I felt betrayed by Jo's infidelity. In truth, I did not, and was never angry with her for an act which I fully recognised to be out of character. Indeed, I am fairly certain she was unfaithful to me because it was the one way she could think of to bring our marriage to a swift and final end.

I empathise with Jo's desire to get rid of me. Any good I had to offer – as a father and a provider – was certainly outweighed by an extremely difficult personality. I was appallingly dismissive and, on principle, disapproved of any initiative Jo took.

'What is it?' I sneered.

I had come home to find her fussing in an excited way over a strange piece of painted furniture. I resented her enthusiasm.

'Heaven knows. Some sort of a table. I picked it up at an auction. Isn't it fabulous?'

'How much was it?'

'Fifty pounds.'

'It's junk. You were done. And I hate it.'

Under the circumstances, who wouldn't have been disheartened? Especially as I continually changed my mind. The table I detested could instantly become the table I adored. One day I might tell Jo we were broke and harangue her to economise, the next I could be ordering a dozen cases of wine for her birthday party. I was quite capable of setting off for work in the morning having made it clear that I did not want Jo to pursue a particular course of action, only to express profound irritation in the evening that she had taken me at my word. A psychic would have been at pains to keep up with my shifting views and opinions, so it is hardly surprising Jo was frustrated. I attempted to regulate every aspect of our lives, too. The house had to be cleaned in the correct way, meals had to be eaten at a specific hour, rooms had to be used for defined purposes.

'How many times have I to ask you, Jo, not to move the television into the drawing room? I can't bear having it in there.'

'But it is the cosiest place to sit.'

It would have been stranger if Jo hadn't wished to escape.

'It is the law,' Jo insisted repeatedly when I challenged her subsequent claim to our house, its contents, half my other assets and an income for life. 'You married me and I intend to get what I am entitled to.'

She openly admitted that she was taking advantage of me, using our son for personal gain. If I wanted access to Nat then I had to pay for it. Until I accepted the inevitable trade-off she was not ashamed to involve him.

In a letter from Australia, my father showed an unexpected confidence in my ability to cope: 'I was dreadfully sorry to hear about you and Jo. It must come as an awful blow to be apart from Nattie – though I am sure it won't stop you from being an excellent parent to the boy.' I wasn't so sure.

'A small packet of Pampers, some wipes and a tub of barrier cream, please.'

I spoke nervously, half expecting the shop assistant to ask me what I wanted with such stuff, anyway, as we both knew I had ample supplies at home and wasn't due to see Nat for another week at the soonest. If I had been a teenager requesting suppositories or condoms I probably couldn't have looked more embarrassed.

'Boy or girl? What size?'

'Boy. The largest size.' I smiled weakly.

'Do you want a bag for the nappies or will you use the handle.'

A bag for the nappies? The whole point of buying the nappies was to be able to parade down the street with them in full view. To declare to the world, 'I am a proud, capable, loving, nappy-buying father.' Shopping for Nat was one of the few ways in which I could reduce my sense of grief. Children's paraphernalia fascinated me. I spent hours examining pushchairs in John Lewis, booster seats in Mothercare, musical potties in Boots. To choose and purchase something for my son was a validation, proof that he existed.

I saw pitifully little of him. I was allowed Wednesday afternoons and alternate weekends. Until he started going to school there wasn't any official provision for holidays. Occasionally Jo would have a crisis and call upon me at short notice to take him for a day or two, and once, when she was in hospital, for longer.

'It is clear she thinks I am just as capable of caring for him as she is.' Spoken calmly.

'Why shouldn't I be the one to have custody? I am as much his parent, after all.' Stated firmly.

'There must be some way to see more of him. There simply must be. I refuse to take no for an answer.' Howled at the top of my voice.

'I am afraid, Jonathan, you would be wasting your money.'

I was on to my third solicitor before I accepted the inevitability of the access arrangements.

At least I could try to make every minute with Nat count. While he was a toddler, Wednesdays were the most difficult. I didn't have sufficient time to make it worth taking him all the way to where I was living, but I had more time (especially in winter) than either of us wished to pass in a playground. On a cold, wet weekday four hours' hanging around in public places with a small child can be a peculiarly bleak experience. After experimenting with museums, libraries and railway stations we found that the Waldorf Hotel suited us best. I brought books, toys and crayons and we curled up with them on a sofa before taking tea. Afterwards we ran races and played games with the waiters in the Palm Court.

Weekends were considerably better, but still a problem. I could never entirely forget that I had to squeeze all my parenting into a mere forty-eight hours. From the second I picked Nat up on Friday evening to the second I dropped him home on Sunday night, the poor boy was subjected to intensive, concentrated, undiluted fathering. It was largely just Nat and me. I simply couldn't bring myself to share him. Nor could I stop myself from making too much of an effort.

'What is this stuff again, Dad?' A perplexed Nat looked at his plate with palpable disgust.

'I cooked it myself.'

'Yes. But what is it?'

'It is called Boeuf Wellington, that's a gratin of butternut squash and those are Dauphin potatoes.'

'I like it when you make me fish fingers.'

Neither of us wished to waste any of our precious time together with arguments.

'I do think you are wrong, Dad,' Nat once said during a row when he was a little older, 'but I'd prefer to drop the whole subject because you have to take me home soon.'

Such disagreements as we had ended abruptly. We were working against the clock and it was impossible to avoid a slightly forced, hurried feel to whatever we did. On a typical Saturday we might have breakfast, play, walk along the canal to the zoo, look at the animals, have a picnic lunch, take a boat out on Regent's Park lake, visit a playground, do some painting, have supper, slosh about in the bath, and read for an hour on my bed. Sundays were, if anything, busier as, driven by the thought that I was about to lose my son again, I struggled to show him by practical means how much he was loved. Invariably he arrived back at his mother's home exhausted.

'I want to stay with you. I want to go home with you.'

In what was now Jo's hall, Nat would cling to me and cling to me until eventually his mother, her boyfriend and I were forced to prise him off. It was the one thing I felt sorry for Jo over, having to deal with Nat's distress after I had gone. My sympathy, however, was short-lived.

151

'Give Mummy more money. She needs more money. Please, Dad.'

I was ringing Nat – as I did every evening – to discuss his day, read him a story and wish him goodnight. In the background his mother was whispering instructions.

'Dad, can you hear what I am saying?'

'Yes, darling, of course.'

'Will you do it?'

'Well, it isn't as simple as that.'

Additional whispered instructions.

'Yes, it is. Just give her more money. Got to go. 'Bye, Dad.'

For a split second her voice comes on.

'You heard him, see. Give me more money.'

Before I could reply the receiver had been replaced.

If I had had a gun I'm not certain that I wouldn't have gone to Brixton, killed Jo, killed her boyfriend, killed Nat and then killed myself. I certainly fantasised about it. She deserved to die because of what she was doing to Nat and me. Her boyfriend deserved to die, not because I was jealous of him and Jo, but because several times Nat had called me Nick instead of Dad and I couldn't bear the thought of another man becoming close to my son. The idea of Nat dying, of my pressing the barrel of a gun against the side of his head and pulling the trigger, was too ghastly to contemplate. However, it seemed unavoidable. His life would be ruined by the death of his mother. And, if I did it while he was asleep hopefully he wouldn't feel any pain. I longed to die, so that part didn't trouble me. I understand completely how men do the terrible things you read about in the papers: murder their families; kidnap their children; disappear for ever; commit suicide. I considered all these options and there were long periods when they struck me as infinitely preferable to the position I was in.

You'll have to go to moose school

'I have to have an abortion.'

Perrie stood irresolutely in the study doorway. I was stretched out on the red sofa reading. It was a Saturday afternoon in early August 1986. A weekend without Nat.

'Sorry?' Absorbed by my book, I assumed I had misheard her.

'I have to have an abortion.'

I got up quickly, letting the book fall to the floor. 'What do you mean?'

'I said I have to have an abortion. I am pregnant, Jonathan.'

My heart leapt. I took her in my arms and pulled her towards me, but her body remained rigid.

'Here,' I spoke urgently, steering her into the bedroom and climbing on to our huge bed, 'come and lie down.'

She hesitated. I tugged at her hand and reluctantly she joined me, but facing in the other direction. I did my best to embrace her.

'You don't have to,' I whispered, 'unless you want to.'

She began to cry. I experienced a surge of anger towards the people in Perrie's past who had conditioned her to think in such a way, vowed that I would never let her down.

'We will have the baby and become a family.'

She stopped crying. Eventually, she turned to look at me.

'You mean you don't want me to have an abortion?'

'Most definitely not.'

153

We might not have planned her pregnancy but it was no accident either. I longed to father another child, and I was determined Perrie would be the mother.

Perrie had no understanding of what she was up against. The moment Will mentioned her existence, I resolved she would be mine.

'She's a journalist on the *Financial Times*. Bright. Australian. Witty. Attractive. I don't know, you'll have to see for yourself. She is invited for dinner on Sunday. Penny thinks you'll like her.'

I liked the idea of her, and that was enough. Before we had even been introduced, I had quite decided it would be love at first sight. My policy from the out was to overwhelm her. I rushed her through the initial stages of courtship at break-neck speed by means of an intensive – if traditional – campaign of flowers and candlelit dinners, chocolates and love letters. When she weakened, I pressed home my advantage with breakfast in bed, expensive jewellery, lifts to work and weekends in country house hotels.

Despite succumbing, she demonstrated a healthy scepticism. 'We aren't really compatible, Jonathan.'

'Yes, we are.'

'The sum total of my desire is an ordinary, quiet, middle-class existence. A good marriage, healthy children, a suburban house, nice friends, an annual holiday and a peaceful old age. Give me a husband who enjoys DIY and I'll be content.'

'I love you, Perrie. I love you, I love you, I love you.'

'Be serious. We have such dissimilar interests. You can't abide opera or ballet. You never make anything with your hands. You won't watch a film with subtitles or an unhappy ending. You refuse to eat foreign food – unless one counts pasta. You don't like pubs, or dancing, or parties, or,' she cast around for a word which epitomised the quintessential nature of our differences, 'or fun. It is no good, Jonathan. You don't like fun.'

There was a considerable amount of truth in this. I didn't do fun at all well. The more fun other people were having, the more unhappy I felt. I simply couldn't let go.

I lay in bed listening. Perrie and her friend from Australia, Lynnie, were in the kitchen which was separated from the bedroom by a long hallway. Both doors were closed but I could sense, if not actually hear them, chattering away as they enjoyed a bottle of whisky and a late night game of cards.

I strained to make out what they were saying.

Intermittently I raised my head from the pillow and sniffed hard. Cigar smoke. How could Perrie allow Lynnie to smoke when she was fully aware that I abhorred the smell? It was infuriating. I looked at the alarm clock for the umpteenth time. Twenty to one in the morning. Perrie knew I wouldn't go to sleep until she came to bed and yet she persisted in sitting up. Finally, twitching with indignation, I threw back the covers and leapt from the bed. Forgetting that I was naked, I wrenched open the bedroom door and stormed down the hallway. At the last moment, remembering my state of undress, I grabbed a scarf from a chair. Holding it over my genitalia, I pressed my shoulder to the kitchen door and burst in.

'Hi, Jonathan,' said Lynnie, somewhat taken aback by my sudden entrance.

I ignored her. 'Are you ever coming to bed?' I demanded of Perrie. She pushed some matchsticks across the table.

'Raise you five, Lynnie.'

'Well, are you coming to bed?'

She glanced up, casually, as if just noticing me. 'Do you have any idea how ridiculous you look?'

Lynnie snickered. I fumed. Perrie turned back to the card game.

'That's Lynnie's scarf you've got wrapped around your midriff, by the way. Please fold it neatly when you're finished with it.'

Slamming and banging, I made my way back to the bedroom.

On another occasion, I became so frustrated with Perrie that I hit her. I punched her quite hard on the chest. Having done so, I left the flat and drove around London for several hours before stopping at a call box to phone her.

'Perrie?'

'What do you want?'

'I am sorry, Perrie, you have no idea how sorry I am.' I began to weep.

'It's not on, Jonathan. It is just not on.'

'I'm sorry, Perrie. I am truly, truly sorry. Please forgive me. I am so sorry.'

I continued to weep.

After an eternity she spoke. 'Where are you?'

'I am not sure. Dartford, I think.'

'Well, you'd better come home so we can talk about it.'

When I got back, red-eyed and puffy-faced, she made me hot chocolate and put me to bed.

'If you ever hit me again, ever, so much as the lightest tap, I will leave you. There will be no second chance.'

We had started living together, at my suggestion, exactly six days after Will's dinner party. I had the rest of our lives completely mapped out. In the short term week nights were to be spent at her flat and weekends at my house. In the medium term, say two or three months, we would sell both places and pool our resources. In the longer term, perhaps a year, Perrie would become pregnant.

'Don't you think we might be rushing it, Jonathan?'

'No.'

I was absolutely convinced we were meant for one another.

When she raised objections I countered them with passionate declarations of my love. Against her better judgement she allowed herself to be swept along by my fervour.

'It is our destiny,' I enthused, spelling out our future, 'we'll have children and a cottage in the country and a garden and a dog and –'

'Oh, you are such an idiot.'

I saw no reason why Perrie and Nat should not be introduced immediately. The first weekend after I had met Perrie, I told Nat about her on the way back to my house in King's Cross.

'Oh,' was his response, 'can we have pizza for supper, please?'

Perrie came over the following morning, looking extremely nervous.

'How old did you say he was?' she whispered when I went out to greet her.

'Three.'

In an effort to help them bond, I suggested she take him for an ice-cream and then to the automatic car wash.

'I've never been responsible for a child before,' she protested.

'It's only for half an hour. He loves the car wash. It will be a breeze.'

'Suppose something happens?'

'Nothing will happen.'

They returned in silence. Nat and the interior of the car were covered with ice-cream. Perrie appeared mildly traumatised.

'How did it go?'

'Fine,' she said through gritted teeth.

Later, when I tucked Nat in, I explained that Perrie would be sleeping with me.

'OK.'

157

'You can snuggle into my bed in the middle of the night like you usually do. She won't mind.'

'OK.'

He must have minded, though, because he chose never to come into my bed again.

Nat and Perrie were on polite but distant terms. I monopolised his care, which suited Perrie, who, by her own admission, lacked any maternal instincts towards Nat. I was pleased if someone assumed Perrie was Nat's mother. She was not so happy about it.

'He isn't mine,' she repeatedly intoned when the three of us went anywhere, 'he's my boyfriend's.'

Perrie announced she was pregnant on a Saturday about ten months into our relationship and on the Sunday I rang Jo and asked if we could, as a special treat, take Nat out to lunch. Walking to the restaurant with him perched on my shoulders, I gave him the news. He was so delighted that he forced me to put him down in order that he could hug Perrie. Wreathed in smiles, he grasped her legs and squeezed for all his might.

'You aren't Daddy's girlfriend. You're my new brother's – or sister's – mummy.'

For Nat it was as if the mystery of Perrie's presence in our lives had been solved. Now that he understood her purpose he treated her with genuine affection. He drew her pictures, reached for her hand when crossing the road, asked her to cut up his food, climbed on to her lap for cuddles. She did her best to reciprocate. Dutifully she knitted him a Thomas the Tank Engine sweater, baked him cookies, read him stories, took him to the playground. To me, however, she was brutally honest.

'The thing is, I don't like Nat and I don't love him. Don't worry. It won't stop me from doing what's right by the boy. I just wanted you to know.'

I brushed it off, as I brushed off so much of what Perrie said.

'All you ever do is work.'

'I don't.'

I did, though. I left for my office at six in the morning, working through until Perrie finished at nine in the evening. I'd pick her up from the *Financial Times*, take her out to dinner, and afterwards settle down at the dining-room table to work some more. On weekends I worked early and late while Perrie and Nat were asleep. I also developed the habit of carrying small pieces of work about with me for when I had a few minutes free. On holiday the most important item of my luggage was a briefcase.

'I'll buy you any outfit of your choosing, anything at all, no matter what it costs, if you manage to have the baby before eight o'clock.'

'What? So that –' a contraction forced Perrie to break off mid-sentence. She groaned and dug her fingernails into my wrist. 'So that you can get to the office when it opens?'

I tried to make a joke of it.

'Nonsense. I've arranged for my secretary to pop in here and take dictation if you're still in labour at nine-thirty.'

I don't imagine she was fooled. As the events of the night had unfolded she probably guessed that more than once my mind had strayed to thoughts of work. Oh, I dealt manfully with inexperienced doctors and obstreperous midwives, stroked Perrie's forehead and whispered words of encouragement, kissed her and sponged her and told her I loved her. I meant it, too. But all the time my eye had been on the clock. Calculating. Allowing an hour for washing and weighing the baby, thirty minutes for getting home, three hours for sleep, forty-five minutes for getting up and into the office, providing she has the baby by six I can be at work before nine-thirty. If I only sleep an hour and a half and she has the baby by seven I can be at work before nine-fifteen. If I don't bother to go to bed, just drop in at home for a shower and a bowl of cereal, so long as she has the baby by eight, I can be at work before nine forty-five.

Then Jack was born. I was thrilled. Ecstatic. Yet even as I cradled him in my arms and the tears of joy ran down my cheeks, across my jaw, and fell gently on to his face, I was thinking: seven-forty, with a fair wind I'll make it to the office before ten.

Perrie and I fought. I was a perpetual disappointment to her. 'You promised you would collect the car from the garage'; 'You promised you would keep that night free for us'; 'You promised you would be home for dinner.'

Our quarrels were, however, largely one-sided. Having voiced her grievance, she would fall silent and ignore me. I, on the other hand, would become worked up, vehemently denying whatever charges she laid against me regardless of their patent validity. 'I am not inconsistent about money'; 'I am not controlling'; 'I am not thoughtless.'

Aware that I dare not risk the slightest act of violence against her person, I confined myself to breaking objects.

'I do wish', she would remark after I had calmed down and we had made up, 'you could learn to control your temper.'

A few months after Jack's birth in 1987 I started to take cocaine on a regular basis. Initially it had a rather beneficial result.

'Are you having an affair, Jonathan?'

'Don't be ridiculous.'

'You seem much chirpier.'

'I have you. I have the boys. Who could want for anything else?'

I saw no reason to explain the cause of my improved demeanour to Perrie. Was it any of her concern if I was self-medicating?

'Are you sure you aren't having an affair?'

'Hand on heart, I swear I have never been unfaithful to you.'

Ironically, just as I began to take hard drugs, Will was giving up.

Far from discouraging Will's passion for drugs, my mother had actively promoted it. While he was still at school she propagated marijuana for his use – deriving considerable amusement from the thought that she was engaging in an illegal activity. Later, when he was at university, she had given him extra money to support his habit.

'He'll grow out of it. I am sure it's just a phase.'

As Will's behaviour became increasingly disturbed she acknowledged her mistake.

'He is an addict. My son is an addict, and it is all my fault.'

With her usual zeal she set about researching the topic – reading, talking to specialists, investigating support groups. If she had erred in encouraging his dependency, she now tried to make up for it. Will was packed off to a rehabilitation clinic and, on his return, his movements were closely monitored. My mother began to attend Families Anonymous meetings.

'You should come,' she enthused, 'you would enjoy it.'

I declined.

I began snorting cocaine well before breakfast and continued hourly until bedtime when I used a combination of valium, marijuana and alcohol to bring myself down. Some nights I was so wired that I couldn't sleep at all. Instead I'd lie in bed attempting to stop my body from going into spasms – terrified that my convulsions would wake Perrie. The more cocaine I consumed, the more I required to achieve a state of normalcy. It became harder and harder to get high. My dealer, who had been a friend long before supplying me with drugs, was aghast at the quantities I was buying and suggested I should ease off.

'Don't worry, only a tiny percentage of this is for me,' I lied. 'I pass it on to colleagues.'

It was hell. For over two years nothing mattered to me except that white powder. My mother knew nothing of my addiction, of course. I prided myself on being better than she was at hiding secrets, though in the end she proved me wrong.

I had thought I had known every object in her flat. That there could have been two large cardboard boxes tucked out of sight in such a small space seems nigh on impossible. The obvious location for them would have been the ceiling-height cupboard in her bedroom. Yet I had rummaged through that cupboard on several occasions and I was familiar with its contents: Nick's antique ceremonial sword; his Mexican poncho; a hideously ugly brass elephant (a gift from one of my father's foreign students); a pile of fabric remnants; a bin-liner bursting with my mother's unwanted clothes; a broken desk lamp; other assorted detritus that she was hoarding for some reason known only to herself. I can picture each item quite clearly. Really, there were so few places where she could have kept them. They certainly weren't at the back of the only wardrobe; in the kitchen; in Will's old room; on any of the bookcases; in the drawers of her desk; in the space under the stairs – for in the past I had searched all those places, too. I wonder whether they were in the flat at all? Perhaps she had been keeping them somewhere else and had only brought them back to the flat when she became unwell.

As she lay dying in her bed, Will and Nick unearthed two large cardboard boxes packed with an assortment of exercise books and began to read from them. They were our mother's diaries, written sporadically over a fifty-year span.

'You shouldn't be going through them. It is wrong.' They sat side by side on the sofa, picking exercise books out at random, speed-reading for anything which might prove revelatory, tossing them aside after a few minutes in their rush to find more exciting material.

'Nonsense,' said Will, barely looking up, 'she is beyond caring now.'

'They are private,' I insisted.

'If she didn't want us to read them she had plenty of time to destroy them,' Nick pointed out, putting his hand back into the box.

'I am looking for 1980. The year she came to visit us in Siena. She took against a pair of jeans which Anna had and objected to her wearing them in public. One day we found the jeans on the floor with holes cut out of them. Mother claimed that someone else had done it with nail scissors, but we were fairly certain it was her. I'll be interested to see if she mentions the incident.'

Will wasn't listening. He was intent on his reading. Suddenly he snorted. 'Did you know she slept with her friend Jane's husband? Fred?'

'Really,' said Nick, 'read me the entry.'

I went through to my mother's bedroom. The nurse, who had been sitting in the corner, got up to greet me and the movement woke my mother. I could quite clearly hear Will reading about the affair with Fred even though the door was closed. My mother was blinking furiously, trying to focus. She began to jerk her head from side to side on the pillow. When she caught sight of me, the jerking suddenly stopped.

'Oh. Johnny? You are here.' The emphasis placed on the 'you' – as if surprised.

Before I could reply she had closed her eyes again and was snoring. Without her false teeth whole sections of my mother's face appeared to be missing. As she inhaled, she sucked the flesh of her cheeks into her mouth and chewed on it. I thought, the cancer is eating her; she is eating herself. As she exhaled it was with such force that I wondered if her flesh might tear. I sat on the edge of her bed, watching in horror for as long as I could bear it, smiled weakly at the nurse and quietly left the room.

We divided our mother's illness and death between us. I received the greater part of her illness, and it looked for a while as if I might get the lot, but at the last moment my brothers stepped in and took over her death. In retrospect I realise that she was ill when she came to stay with Perrie and me in the country over Christmas 1987 – for even by her standards she was particularly bad tempered – but it wasn't until late January that she announced the cancer.

'I'll beat it,' she said with conviction, 'it is just a matter of positive thinking.'

Despite the fact that she found the treatment incredibly debilitating, she wouldn't let me take her for her chemotherapy sessions at University College Hospital. However, under pressure, she did accept the services of a driver. It was the same with her daily care. I wasn't permitted to shop, cook or clean for her, but, when it was clear she could no longer manage on her own, she reluctantly allowed me to arrange for someone to help out for a few hours each day. Every evening, after work, I visited her on the way home. Thus I took on responsibility for looking after her through this part of the illness. Will pretty much left it to me to organise things; and Nick stayed in Italy, telephoning daily for the latest report.

She remained relatively cheerful. I don't remember her being angry at the thought of her impending demise, because I don't think she ever acknowledged it, though she was frustrated at not being able to do more. Within a matter of weeks she became bedridden; then too weak to argue about the introduction of agency nurses. Soon afterwards her mind began to drift. Finally, she was transported by ambulance to the hospital.

Everything changed the moment our mother lost the power of coherent speech. It felt as if my brothers had been waiting until they no longer had to converse with her. Nick came from Rome; Will was galvanised into action. With cries of 'It is what she would have wanted,' they took control: staking out the hospital and repelling outsiders; consulting with the doctors and making the medical decisions. Two was company, three was a crowd. Which is why, the night she died, Nick and Will were by her side while I was out wandering the streets. As she drew her last breath I rather suspect I was enrolling for membership of a casino. I became somewhat unbalanced there, at the end.

My brothers argued against a funeral. In among our mother's papers they had found a press cutting about how undertakers overcharged, across which she had written 'Get three quotes', and this seemed sufficient justification to avoid any sort of ceremony. Instead they went alone to the crematorium and came away half an hour later with a plastic bottle containing her ashes. After Nick had gone back to Italy, those ashes provided Will and me with many hours of amusement. We carried Mum with us to the solicitor's office for the signing of all the legal papers relating to her estate; she was taken to a dinner party by Will, who kept her on the mantelpiece; and I sent postcards and left telephone messages for her. We discussed bringing her for a nice Sunday afternoon drive when the weather became warmer. Since we couldn't agree where our mother's ashes should be scattered, she remained a tangible presence in our lives for several years after her death. At one point, when Will moved house, she went with the furniture to a place in White City called – appropriately enough – Self Storage. Many years later, Will, our nephew Robin, and I attempted to bury her in Kenwood. It was a windy day and the bits of Mum that didn't get blown away largely attached themselves to our trousers and shoes.

I feel immense compassion and sympathy for my mother. But I don't miss her. When my hair receded, scars from where she had hit me became clearly visible and I took a perverse delight in showing them off to people. Will always has to remind me of the date she died: 6 April 1988.

My life during these years could be defined as a series of trips to my dealer; a series of trips to the lavatory where with shaking hands I would hurriedly crush the little crystals of cocaine, arrange them in two untidy lines, roll up a banknote and – eyes watering from the pain – ingest. Every waking moment was devoted to obtaining the drug, hiding it, devouring it, concealing its effects. I lived in dread of being without it. I lived in dread of being discovered. I lived with the expectation that it would kill me. In the end, to satisfy my craving, I had to snort such large quantities that my face, my mouth, my throat, my lungs were paralysed and I would be forced to gasp for each breath like a drowning man, fearful it would be my last.

It seems extraordinary that no one guessed what was wrong. I can only assume that my behaviour must already have been so strange and unpredictable that the drug made no difference.

A knock on the dining-room door. Quickly I wipe my nose and hide the tissue.

'Yes?'

Perrie bearing a cup of tea. 'It's Saturday, why don't you come and help me in the garden?'

'I've got about another half-hour of work and then I'm done.'

'Half an hour, half an hour. Come now.'

'I'll just finish this.'

'So you say.'

As she is leaving I call after her. 'Thanks for the tea. Could you close the door.'

Ten minutes later another knock. I wipe my nose and hide the tissue. Exasperated I shout, 'Give me a break.'

A timid voice replies, 'It's us, Dad.'

'Oh, for fuck's sake,' under my breath so that they can't hear. I get down on my hands and knees and crawl over to the door.

'Neigh, neigh, whinny,' I call out, 'there's no Dad in here, just a dangerous bucking bronco.'

Nat and Jack titter in nervous anticipation.

'Neeeeeeigh! Do you dare to enter this room for the ride of your lives?'

In they tumble, still in their pyjamas.

I whinny and kick out my back legs. 'Whoooo is first?'

Twenty minutes later Perrie finds us whispering under the dining-room table.

'Nat, I think your horns are coming through.'

'What do you mean, Dad?'

'Your horns. You are turning into a moose.'

'I am not.'

'You are. You'll have to go to moose school.'

'What about my horns?' From a hopeful Jack.

'Your half-hour is up.' From an impatient Perrie.

'It isn't. I've been playing with the kids. Off you go, chaps, so I can finish my work.'

In this manner I persuaded myself that I was not neglecting my boys. For when I compared myself to my father, it seemed to me that I was intimately involved in their upbringing. He hadn't got up in the middle of the night to deal with a teething baby, or rocked a cot for hours to help a toddler go to sleep, or spent a whole afternoon building a castle from cardboard boxes to amuse a six-year-old. But I was aware of my faults. I lost my temper with them.

'Dad?'

'Will you be quiet. I'm bored with telling you.'

'Dad.'

'Will you shut the fuck up?'

'Dad, I am going to throw up.'

I was vague.

'I came third in the relay race at Sports Day.'

'Sorry. What did you say, Jack?'

'I said I came third in the relay race. And I'm Nat.'

'Sorry. Can you wait? I'm a bit tied up at the moment.'

I was emotionally absent.

'Dad, massage my shoulders.'

'Come over here, then.'

'I love you, Dad.'

'I love you, too.'

When what I should have said was 'I want to love you, too,' because no matter how much I did or didn't do for my children, mostly I felt numb inside. Yet I clung doggedly to the belief that I was a good father.

'Actually, you care more about the people you work with than you do about your family.' Perrie spat out the words. 'If we were clients you would pay us more attention.'

'That's not true.'

'No wonder you don't have any friends.'

'That's not true, either.'

'Remind me again how many people there were at your thirtieth birthday party.'

'Mad Cousin Sidney would have come.'

'If the best you can do is Mad Cousin Sidney . . .'

Sidney was my father's second cousin, a confirmed alcoholic who had been arrested en route to my party, in drag, for drunken driving.

'Returning from a vicars and tarts shindig the night before, old chap. Decided I'd just come on. Frightful nuisance. Probably lose my licence. Damn sorry to miss your show.'

Perrie had invited over twenty people to a surprise lunch

at our country place – secretly made the most elaborate preparations – and of the three guests to turn up, two had been employees.

'At least Sidney had the courtesy to telephone,' Perrie sighed.

'Will got the date confused.'

'The date of your birthday? You're in denial, Jonathan.'

Denial permeated every nook and cranny of my being.

Tell me about your dog's hysterectomy

I founded Self Direct, a direct marketing agency, when I was twenty-two. It was by no means my only business – over the years I dabbled in everything from hairdressing to stationery, recruitment to giftware – but it was my main business, where I went each morning. At its peak it employed over a hundred people.

I had never meant to go into advertising. From the age of fourteen my weekend and holiday jobs had been in council-run adventure playgrounds looking after children not so much younger than myself. I planned, on leaving school, to become a social worker. Then, at eighteen, I had moved in with Sarah, my mother's friend from Duckworth Publishing.

'Advertising is much better paid,' Sarah had pointed out, 'and you don't have to stay in it for ever.'

I found a job as a trainee copywriter.

'That's not real writing,' warned my mother.

'Why don't you try your hand at something useful? I would argue that street cleaning is a more honourable activity,' contended my father.

I was horribly precocious and annoyed a string of employers, five in less than two years, but did learn the trade. At twenty I thought I knew enough to set up on my own. I rented an office in Covent Garden, bought a suit at C&A, and put a silver-framed photo of a woman and a baby on my desk, hoping people would think that they were my wife and child, that I was older than I appeared.

'If only I had known that when you jemmy a door it is better to do it on the side of the hinges. I told you we got in through the downstairs door like they do in the movies, using a credit card?'

'Yes, Harry, you did.'

'It was worth a try but I'll have to find a different way of getting the evidence.'

My main client was a solicitor who had sold his legal practice in order to buy a chain of fashion shops. I had been handling his advertising for several months when he admitted he couldn't pay any of my bills and was supplementing his own income by means of what he blithely referred to as 'industrial espionage'.

'Tell you what,' he had said, 'why don't I get you a project to tide you over?'

'Breaking and entering isn't really my field of expertise.'

'Trust me.'

I forget the precise nature of that first project. Something to do with proving that a public company director was in breach of his fiduciary duties. It led on to another project, and another. I discovered that a talent for writing persuasive copy could be turned to other uses.

'I'll be flying in from South Africa,' I explained, 'and suggest a meeting at Heathrow if it would be convenient.'

The man at the other end of the telephone was believed to have stolen some newly developed software and was looking for financial backing to start his own operation. I was to receive a substantial cash sum plus expenses if I obtained his business plan, and a bonus if he gave me a copy of the software.

'Yes, that would be fine.'

He sounded keen. I had led him to believe that I represented

171

a syndicate of rich South Africans with 'hot' money looking for overseas investments.

'I'll have a hotel room booked so that we aren't disturbed. My chauffeur will pick you up outside the Departures area of Terminal Three at one o'clock. He'll be in a black Daimler Sovereign.'

The chauffeur was booked by the hour from a limousine firm and I wasn't flying in from South Africa, only coming by Tube from the East End. Through trial and error I had found that Heathrow was one of the best places to hold this sort of meeting. It was anonymous, inexpensive and somehow conjured up the right sort of image. Appearances counted for everything in the game I was playing, especially as I was so young. I knew that it was the small circumstantial details which convinced my targets I was on the level. That and their greed.

'You do understand that this is South African money?' I asked him. 'You have no objections to apartheid?' I doubted he knew what apartheid was. He hesitated.

'No, no. None whatsoever. We just require funding, Mr Self.'

'Good. I look forward to hearing more.'

I rang off before he could say goodbye.

At the appointed hour he was collected by the chauffeur and an actor posing as my bodyguard, driven to the hotel, taken up to a penthouse suite, frisked for weapons, and then brought through to meet me. The supposed bodyguard stood to attention waiting for instructions.

'Clean, sir.'

'OK. You can go now, Brown. I'll call for you if I want you.'

'Yes, sir.'

I turned to my guest. 'Sorry for that. I carry a lot of cash and have to be careful. Anyway, thank you for coming. Let me tell you a little about myself and the people I represent . . .'

It took me twenty-two minutes to get his business plan, and a further twelve minutes to get the software specification. As he was in the process of handing over the second document, I interrupted him and called the phoney bodyguard back into the room. I needed a witness.

'Brown, I'll require you in a moment.'

'Yes, sir,' said Brown.

'Sorry, please do go on. Now tell me again what this technical document you are giving me is.'

Dutifully he repeated what he had been saying. Later the actor and I would both report the gist of the conversation to a lawyer who, in turn, would prepare affidavits for us to sign.

'And you are only looking for one hundred and fifty thousand?' I asked him.

He licked his lips. 'Yes.'

'And you can prove that this software cost over a million pounds to develop?'

'Yes.'

'Well, I'll take it back to South Africa and if they agree with me that it is worth serious consideration they'll probably want you to fly out next week. Would that be a problem?'

'No. I am completely free next week.'

I suppressed an urge to say that next week he would probably be answering questions in a police station and instead asked him if my driver could drop him anywhere.

It was my notoriety in the rather murky world of corporate security – once I had begun, the referrals and recommendations flowed in – and not my proficiency as a copywriter that funded my increasingly expensive tastes.

However, I was never comfortable living on the proceeds of what was, albeit perfectly legal, deceit. I was grateful when Self Direct took off and I could afford to stop.

Self Direct yo-yoed in and out of profit. A year of phenomenal growth would be followed by a year spent teetering on the verge of bankruptcy. Up or down, one thing I tried to avoid was discussing its fortunes with my family.

My father lectured me: 'If you must involve yourself in these dubious commercial undertakings, you should at least give away all the money you make. Take my pal, Tennant. He made a killing in property before he was thirty and then devoted himself to the creation of low-cost housing.'

My brother, Will, taunted me: 'What does it feel like to be the UK's most prolific writer of junk mail? To know that every year thousands of beautiful trees are destroyed, and more of the world's fragile ozone layer depleted, solely to satisfy your lust for stuffing our letterboxes with useless and binable offers? Could your enormous girth and follicly challenged pate be caused by the remotest sensation of remorse? Come on, do tell.'

Not only did I feel guilty about my career, I hated it. The more I despised what I was doing, the more successful my agency seemed to become. The more successful the agency, the greater my disdain. Privately I agreed with my father and Will. Direct marketing served no useful purpose and was morally questionable. Worse, it was boring.

'We'll roll out the current control with the scratch-off involvement devices in January'; 'Test cell three, the one with the colour envelope, showed a significant uplift of a quarter of a per cent'; 'There are thirteen different items in this mailing pack and I'd like to take you through each of them in detail.'

For outright tedium it is hard to beat direct marketing. There are those, I know, who become excited about laser printing and response rates, free calculators and postal discounts. I do not rank among their number. My years in the industry were spent professing a level of enthusiasm I did not feel.

Then there were the clients: predominantly difficult, unimaginative, ungrateful and humourless types. There were exceptions, naturally, and I flatter myself that Self Direct managed to attract an above-average percentage of them. On the whole, however, it was heavy going.

Although I never stopped writing copy my real skill lay in persuading clients to use our services. Early on I came to understand that growing the business had less to do with marketing expertise (we were no better or worse than any of our competitors) and everything to do with developing personal relationships. In this I was my mother's son – a past master at identifying and exploiting a client's needs, priorities and motivations.

If they were ambitious, I helped them to plot. 'It is imperative that you become marketing director and I have a number of ideas to ensure your victory.'

If they were greedy, I was generous. 'I was in Asprey's and saw this. A small token of my appreciation for your business.'

If they were in trouble, I comforted them. 'What a sad story. You've been through the mill, all right.'

If they were lonely, I befriended them. 'You were halfway through telling me about your dog's hysterectomy.'

My objective was to tie them to me, make them dependent, and I wasn't above enrolling my family in the task. 'I was wondering if you and your children would like to come and stay for the weekend? Our boys are about the same age as yours.' I would say anything to ingratiate myself with a client. 'What a fascinating hobby. I've long nurtured a yearning to become a train spotter.'

I complied with every demand my clients made of me. I worked all night, worked all weekend, neglected my family, neglected myself, to ensure that my clients were always satisfied. Moreover, I did it with a smile on my lips. Clients do not like to hear that you have been put out or that they are being unreasonable. They want to see happy, compliant faces around them.

I may have been a chameleon, camouflaging myself according to the likes and dislikes of whoever I was dealing with, but I wasn't entirely a sycophant.

'You're not treating us fairly,' I snapped at a client when he began to give me the runaround. 'We've done first-class work for you and we deserve the rest of your business.'

Nor was I a total hypocrite. One Christmas I sent an outstandingly odious client a penis expander with a card that read: 'So you can become an even bigger prick next year.'

'Why not switch career? You are still extremely young.' Perrie, knowing how much I abhorred what I was doing, encouraged me to give it up.

I couldn't. To begin with, there was the money. 'From copywriting alone I can earn, in a couple of days, more than the average national salary for an entire year. And I can't keep up with the demand.'

I was not immune to a mawkish pride, either. My agency won industry awards. I was quoted in the national media. I was invited to speak at international conferences. Most relevant of all, 'What else can I do? I'm not qualified for anything else.'

Self Direct's client list was remarkably blue chip – we handled direct marketing for organisations such as American Express, British Telecom, the *Financial Times*, Next and Norwich Union – given my unconventional staffing policy. Vacancies were filled entirely by word of mouth; jobs were given to those in want regardless of their ability; eccentricity was certainly no bar to employment.

'Can I help you?'

'Yes, my name is Flint, I've got a meeting with Mr Self.'

'That's wonderful. Absolutely wonderful.' Freddy sprang up and gave Mr Flint a bear hug. 'Welcome. Welcome to Self Direct.'

'Freddy,' I said, coming out of my office, 'let go of Mr Flint, please.'

Freddy was one of our receptionists. At the time I put his habit of hugging visitors down to misplaced enthusiasm. After he left I discovered he was on ecstasy. I led a flustered Mr Flint to the boardroom. Happily Bret, my personal assistant, was in the character of an English butler that particular day.

'May I fetch you and your guest some light refreshment, sir?'

Sometimes Bret, a resting actor, was John Wayne. On other occasions Jimmy Stewart. He did a good Marilyn Monroe, too.

'Herf-direc, chan-I-chelp-oo?' Fara, our switchboard operator, was Iranian and spoke English with an impenetrable accent. Stephanie, who was in charge of the artwork studio, brought four ancient and incontinent Labradors to work with her. George, an art director, was agoraphobic and operated from one of the lavatory cubicles. Tony, the Indian bookkeeper, was learning Yiddish. Don, the creative director, had a clutch of former rent boys (including a transvestite) managing his department. Mitch, the production supervisor, was stripping down a racing-car engine in our kitchen. Kim, an account director, believed the end was nigh and peppered his conversation with dire warnings of eternal damnation. The cleaner was an amateur boxer called Hector the Hammer who longed to be put in charge of credit control. There was a perpetual shortage of secretarial support, but we did engage the full-time services of a poet.

I was driven by a single, burning ambition. To sell Self Direct for a sufficiently large sum never to have to work again.

Untruths, half-truths, bent truths and inventions

'Good God, Jonathan. What are you doing up at this hour?'

Perrie twisted around in bed and watched me getting dressed. It was six-thirty.

'Breakfast meeting in London.'

'You didn't say anything yesterday.'

'Sorry, I forgot.'

'Who are you going to see?'

'Possible client.'

Perrie sat bolt upright.

'What? Tell me you are kidding.'

'He has been calling and calling. I couldn't resist. It is huge.'

'You told me that contractually you weren't allowed to work in advertising again for at least five years.'

At the age of thirty I had sold Self Direct and, in theory, was now retired.

'I've thought of a way around it. Anyhow, I haven't won the account, so don't fret.'

I didn't know how to fill my time, now that I was no longer working. When friends asked: 'What are you doing now?' I would reply moodily, 'I have retired. I'm just staying home, hanging out with my family, taking holidays.'

Over the course of a few months I drifted back to precisely what I had been doing before the sale. It wasn't a conscious decision. I started a new advertising agency, schmoozed clients, wrote copy and – on the side – invested in even more small businesses without once considering why I was returning to a way of life I loathed. I was certainly under no financial obligation to do so, at least initially.

My father reclined in his deckchair, lit a cigar and gazed dreamily up at the sky. We were on a terrace overlooking the lawn. My housekeeper had just finished clearing away the table after lunch. Below us, some little way off, Perrie toiled over an herbaceous border and Jack played with his nanny.

'I can't tell you how delighted I am to see you restoring the family fortunes. Must take oodles of the stuff to keep this place up and running. How many gardeners do you have?'

'Right now? Two.'

'You must be doing incredibly well.'

Neither the admiration nor the jealousy I detected in his voice brought me any satisfaction.

'Perrie would like us to lead a simpler, less lavish lifestyle. She isn't comfortable with all this.'

'Easy for her to say.'

'I think she means it. She is embarrassed turning up to Friends of the Earth meetings in a Bentley.'

'Let her try being poor for a change.'

'She has, and I gather she preferred it.'

The subject was one to which Perrie and I frequently returned.

'What's it all for, Jonathan? Why do we need it?'

'Why not? If we've got the money?'

'But do we have the money?'

With her usual perspicacity Perrie had hit upon the crux of the issue. Regardless of how much I earned, and I earned a great deal, I was always short of cash. My wild extravagance aside, I could never resist a hard-luck story.

'There's close to a three-year wait on the NHS. Howard may not last that long and if he does he's unlikely to be well

179

enough for the operation. We looked at going private, but at ten thousand pounds it is out of the question. Our only hope is that he can jump the queue.'

Margaret, Howard's wife, was one of our former cleaners. We'd employed her for perhaps a year. Driving past their cottage, entirely by chance, I had dropped in for a cup of tea.

I didn't hesitate. 'If you have had no joy in, say, six months, let me know and I'll pay for him to have the operation privately.'

As it happened the NHS came through, but I wasn't short of alternative candidates in need of assistance. The slightest of acquaintances benefited from my largesse.

'You want to visit your sick boyfriend in Greece?' Two hundred pounds for a temporary receptionist.

'Exactly how far behind with your mortgage payments are you?' Eighteen hundred pounds for a single-parent neighbour.

'What will it cost to make the car roadworthy, then?' Four hundred and thirty pounds for the disabled sister of a friend.

I gave as freely of my time as of my money.

'Listen, it's my city. I'll organise a complete itinerary for her, arrange theatre tickets and book some restaurant tables.' A couple of hours on the telephone for a cousin's mother-in-law.

'I'd be pleased to provide a bit of career advice.' An evening of discussion for the daughter of a man I had met on a train.

'Let me write the first draft of your business plan to get you started.' A day at the word processor for my barber.

If other people's troubles were my troubles, then their pain was definitely my pain. Where I couldn't supply a practical solution I could, at least, offer a sympathetic ear. I virtually begged morose-looking strangers to come and cry on my shoulder. I was motivated by empathy, pity, a desire to feel useful, shame at having so much myself. And by something less admirable. My mother once told me: 'As a child, if I was invited to a sleepover, I always rose early the following morning to do housework. I remember one set of parents becoming seriously angry when they woke up to find that I had cleaned and reorganised all their kitchen cupboards.' Her confession highlighted our shared compulsion to provide help regardless of whether it was wanted. There is a point, after all, when the best intentions turn into unwelcome, patronising and inappropriate interference. I wonder, too, if the ceaseless – often excessive – giving might not have been as ostentatious in its way as, say, my employing a domestic staff of five to care for a family of three.

'If you didn't adopt such a feckless approach to money, if you saved, you wouldn't have to work so hard. If you didn't have to work so hard we could spend more time together.'

Perrie's logic contained a single flaw: I didn't want to work less hard and I didn't want to spend more time with her. This had nothing to do with Perrie and everything to do with me. I chose to keep myself obscenely busy. To make certain I never had a spare minute I manufactured extra projects. Opening my journal for 1990 at random, the last week of May finds me in the midst of administering an arts award, overseeing a major property renovation, assisting a distant relative with a complex legal claim and fundraising for a charity – as well as myriad lesser activities such as choosing a wedding present for a colleague and advising a friend on how to switch mortgages. All of which was in addition to extensive work and family commitments.

For someone with such a hectic life, I was remarkably detached from what was going on around me. Perrie's complaint, 'You live in a fantasy world,' may have fallen on deaf ears but was, in essence, accurate. My grasp on reality was often tenuous. If I didn't like what I heard or saw I disregarded it, and produced my own version of events.

'There is no problem', I used to boast, 'so large or disagreeable that it can't be ignored.'

Thus I did nothing about Nat's recurring bouts of depression or our persistent overspending or my doctor's health warnings or a patently disloyal employee. It is why, when Perrie kept saying, 'I am miserable. We must do something to improve our relationship. It is the reason I am always ill,' I barely put down my copy of *Country Life* to reply, 'Our relationship is brilliant. Absolutely fine. You're just a bit under the weather.'

To a large extent my physical presence was meaningless since my mind was invariably engaged elsewhere. I was almost aggressively self-contained. Perrie wasn't being in the least bit unfair when she accused me of 'making it up as you go along'.

I deluded myself into thinking that my falsehoods were harmless: an embellishment to make a story more interesting, a white lie to get out of an unwanted social event, a minor fib to avoid some unpleasantness. On reflection, my entire existence was one long string of untruths and half-truths and bent truths and inventions. I lied about where I was and what I was doing. I lied about money. I lied about my personal circumstances, habits, past, wealth, successes and failures. I lied about being happy. I lied about loving Perrie.

After considerable difficulty I had managed to give up hard drugs. Too proud to seek professional assistance, I cured myself. Time and again I succeeded in staying clean for a week or two, only to relapse. I would visit my dealer and then, disgusted with myself, throw away whatever I had purchased. I have a vivid picture of myself hurling hundreds of pounds' worth of cocaine over the parapet of Waterloo Bridge, collapsing on the pavement in relief at having ridded myself of the wretched narcotic, and then immediately returning to my dealer to purchase some more. I discovered that if I hurt myself the pain served as a distraction. I covered my body with cuts and burns and when my desire for cocaine became unbearable I would rub and pinch them until the yearning left me. It was by this means that ultimately I broke my habit.

Yet, although I was no longer in the grip of that particular addiction, I was hardly stable. I suffered from hair-trigger impatience.

'We've been here precisely seven minutes and we haven't seen the menus.'

'The waitress is fetching our drinks, Jonathan.'

'We could have been looking at the menus while we were waiting.'

'Honestly, Jonathan, we aren't in a rush.'

No one else may have been in a rush, but I was. Before breakfast I wrote out a plan for the day containing an hour-by-hour task list. Until everything I had set out to achieve was completed, I could not rest. I wasn't above providing similar lists for those around me.

'Hi, Perrie. I'm just telephoning to check you contacted the plumber, picked up our tickets for the weekend, and changed the fish-tank water.'

Perrie generally met my neuroses with patient good humour.

'Mate, mate,' she'd say in her slow Australian drawl, 'I'm your partner not your secretary. Anyway, it's only midmorning.'

It wasn't that Perrie didn't have her failings. In a moment of candour she declared: 'I can be resentful. I do get jealous. And my bad moods sometimes last for weeks.' However, compared to mine, her faults paled into insignificance. Heaven knows what redeeming features she thought she saw in me. Exasperated by some aspect of my behaviour she would quietly sigh: 'At least it is never dull being around you. I know you mean well.'

Calculating the misery factor

There was something decidedly surreal about Bert's birth. Like a dream sequence, his mother and I passed effortlessly from sleep to wakefulness, the bedroom to the garage, the house to the hospital, barely exchanging a word. The car seemed to steer itself – gliding through the freezing fog, silent and steady – confident of the route. When we arrived, the hospital was unlit, its car park empty, abandoned. No one to meet us in reception, no one to welcome us in the casualty department. Whispering, shuffling, we slid quietly through the slumbering building in search of the maternity ward – half expecting that this, too, would be deserted.

'You dear, dear man. Did you have to come far?'

'Banham.'

'And at this hour. How long did it take you?'

I consulted my watch.

'Forty-five minutes. I didn't think it wise to drive too fast in this weather.'

'Quite right. Bound to be black ice. Better safe than sorry, I say. Now, who have you brought us?'

'This is Perrie. Perrie Croshaw.'

The matron consulted the list on her clipboard, took out a pen, and carefully drew a line through Perrie's name.

'We've been expecting you,' she said cheerfully. 'If you'd bring your wife this way, Mr Croshaw, I'll follow.'

For a split second I hesitated, wondering if I should correct her error.

'Yes?' The matron had the look of a woman who didn't approve of children being born out of wedlock.

'Nothing.'

I slowly led Perrie, who was leaning heavily on my arm, through a set of swing doors and down a corridor. The matron hovered behind us. Our little procession passed a waiting room. Two nurses were watching satellite television: CNN, news from the Gulf. The volume was up so high that the matron had to raise her voice.

'Next on your left, please, Mr Croshaw.'

We entered a darkened room and stood waiting while the matron fumbled for the switch. The television could be heard quite distinctly through one wall. Exploding bombs and the urgent, staccato chatter of a war correspondent reporting from the front. Through the far wall a different noise. A woman moaning. I could just make out the large and menacing shape of the hospital bed in the gloom. The neon lamp flickered into life, flooding the room with its harsh light. A bare, utilitarian room. Bed. Sink. Trolley. Hard chair. Clothes stand.

'Oh. Oh. Oh. Fuck. Fuck. Fuck. Oh. Oh. Oh,' went the woman.

'Take off your clothes and put on this tunic, dear,' said the matron, addressing Perrie directly for the first time, 'and just pop up on to the bed while I show your husband where he can wait.'

'Actually, I'll be staying with my wife.'

The matron was obviously surprised.

'You don't have to, you know.'

'I'd prefer it. We would both prefer it.'

'Well, I think that's very nice – and very modern – of you. Hold on a tick.'

She shot out of the door and reappeared a minute later with one of the easy chairs from the waiting room. She was followed in by a nurse carrying a coffee table. They arranged the furniture in a corner, trying it in different positions. When the matron was satisfied she turned to me and said, 'You relax, Mr Croshaw, and I'll go and get you some tea and toast. Meantime, Nurse will give your wife a quick check up.'

The matron's briskness, the television, the brightness, the other woman in labour came as a dreadful shock to us. It was as if someone had started shouting in church.

How alien it seemed to steal into this forsaken space in dead of night to share with strangers so intimate a business as a birth. To help Perrie climb, half naked, upon the bed and to watch her carefully putting her feet in the stirrups ready for the big push. To find nurses who appeared more concerned with my welfare than the mother's, who were reluctant to disturb the doctor because he was resting and they didn't want to wake him. To listen through the walls to the unnerving sound of two battles, one each side of us: the screaming woman in labour and the whine of falling missiles. To have the baby arrive with such speed, barely giving me time to drink my tea or eat my toast.

Bert was in a remarkable hurry, right from the start, from three in the morning on 22 January 1991. And I was afraid for him. The world was in turmoil. His mother and I were in turmoil. His future seemed bleak and I felt guilty at having brought him into existence only to suffer.

When Bert was born we were living, for the most part, in a house in Norfolk called the Garden of Eden. We also had a flat in Dublin and what Australians refer to as a hobby farm, south of Sydney. During the eight years of our partnership Perrie and I owned or rented thirteen homes. Our inability to stay in one location was akin to a sickness. As things between us became worse so the distance between our homes became greater and the length of time we spent in each became shorter. It was like some bizarre human equation: divide the number of miles travelled each year by the frequency of your journeys and then multiply the total by the sum of homes inhabited to arrive at the misery factor.

We didn't spend any longer nor were we more settled in the Garden of Eden than anywhere else. However, it cast its spell over each of us so that even Bert, who cannot possibly hold any recollections of the place, speaks of it with awe.

'There was a cave thing.'

'Do you mean the grotto?'

'Perhaps. I remember a pond.'

'There were quite a few ponds and pools.'

'Also lots of hothouses with grapes and peaches. A tunnel with seats in it. A tower. A cannon. A walkway through the treetops. A big orchard. A secret walled garden. Fountains.' Bert described it with absolute certainty as if he were looking at a picture.

'How do you know all this? You were only one.'

'Nat and Jack told me.'

There is another reason why that house, of all our houses, probably features more prominently in the children's memories. I had started to work from home and it was the last place where we functioned as a proper family. Its sale represented the beginning of the end of my relationship with Perrie – and our move to a series of temporary, rented homes.

If Perrie was organising an outing she tended to favour political demonstrations, collecting signatures on petitions and voluntary work. If I was in charge I veered between the extremes of healthy, outdoor pursuits on the one hand, and blatant consumerism on the other. When I herded the children into the car they never knew whether they were headed for a countryside trudge or a spending spree in the nearest toy shop.

Perrie and I had equally differing views when it came to holidays. She favoured guest houses in popular seaside resorts and would, had I not stood firm, have taken us camping. I stuck rigidly to the view that unbridled luxury and twenty-four-hour room service in a warm climate were the hallmarks of a proper break. I bore the scars of childhood holidays in Britain with my father. The mandatory wet weather, nebulous accommodation arrangements, and monotonous car journeys were the least of it. Our itinerary was based around visits to council estates because my father saw holidays as an ideal opportunity to carry out field research for his books on urban and rural planning.

'Isn't that fascinating?'

It was late afternoon and we were on the outskirts of Sheffield. In front of us stretched a neat terrace of redbrick cottages.

'Yes, Dad. Can we go now?'

He pointed with his walking stick.

'What do you note about the layout, Johnny? What does it remind you of?'

I shrugged.

'Come on, we must investigate this.'

He approached the first cottage and before I could protest had knocked smartly on the door. It was opened by a middle-aged woman holding a baby. A boy, not much younger than myself, hid in her skirts.

'Good afternoon.' My father raised his cap. 'I expect you like living here?'

The woman stared in blank incomprehension.

'My name is Peter Self, Professor Peter Self, and I was wondering . . .'

Moments later we were inside and the woman, having given us a guided tour, was making us tea. By which practical means I became conversant with pretty much every style of low-income and public housing built from the reign of Queen Victoria onwards. Other children might compare the relative merits of Brighton and Southend piers. I could compare the relative merits of Peabody Trust buildings in Blackfriars with slum tenements in Glasgow, Arts and Crafts cottages in Letchworth with modern semis in Milton Keynes.

An inherited passion for housing was one of the reasons I never minded visiting Perrie's relatives in Sydney. While they cooed over Jack, and later Bert, I would take Nat off on lengthy suburban rambles.

'You'll note that immigrant Australians invariably choose to construct their dwellings in the mode of their home country.'

'Yes, Dad.'

'Tiny English Tudor cottages cosy up to miniature Mexican haciendas, diminutive Italianate villas rub shoulders with Lilliputian Swiss chalets. Here a modest Swedish lodge, there a small Asian temple.'

'Can we go to that playground, please?'

'If Grandad were here we would be getting ourselves invited inside some of these houses to look around.'

'Can we go to that playground?'

'OK.'

It was impossible not to feel sorry for Nat, and equally impossible to know what could be done to improve his situation. Diagnosed as dyspraxic and dyslexic, at the age of eleven he had been sent away to a boarding school that offered special teaching. Despite the extensive additional coaching he thus received, on a bad day the simplest of activities challenged him – catching a ball, holding a glass, reading a street sign. With remarkable equanimity he allowed himself to be shuttled between various quasi-hostile environments: his mother's, his school and his father's. He adored his younger

Sixteen conversations with or about my children

'It is the practice in Ireland to tie the body to the bed for the duration of the wake so that, when rigor mortis sets in, the corpse is good and straight. Pass the salt, would you?'

'The company's management practice might be described as ready, fire, aim. Oh, just a drop if you insist.'

'Yes, she is still with us. But today is her day off.'

'Which is your favourite Ninja Mutant Hero Turtle?'

Sunday lunch. Perrie, Jack, Bert, half a dozen guests and I on plastic garden chairs squeezed around a makeshift table because the Australian house is not yet fully furnished. One of those sudden, awkward, unexpected breaks in the conversation occurs. For an instant the whole party falls mute, each of us frozen, embarrassed, as if discovered at something we should not be doing. During the silence, which barely lasts five seconds, Perrie says, apparently apropos of nothing in particular, 'Jack. Bert. I have an announcement to make. Your father and I are thinking of separating.'

Before we have a chance to react, the conversation, which has a life of its own, starts up again and sweeps us along in other directions.

'The great trick, when we were kids, was to slip under the bed and cut the ropes because if you got the timing right, the body would suddenly sit up and terrify the mourners rigid.'

'Nasty bunch. They smile you in the back and then stab you in the front. No, I'm on the red.'

'Why do nannies always take up with aerobics instructors?'

'I don't really have a favourite.'

Much later, when the guests have gone and the boys are in bed, Perrie asks, 'What will you do about seeing the children?'

I reply absent-mindedly, 'I'll just come backwards and forwards from Europe. After all, it's only a matter of sitting on a plane.'

We agree that for the time being, when I am in Australia, I'll live in the studio behind the house.

Nat is waiting for me outside the school office. He stands impassively under an orange street lamp, shoulders hunched, hands thrust deep into the pockets of his coat. Although it is dark and drizzling he has his skateboard with him. Nat doesn't go anywhere without his skateboard.

'Hello, darling.'

His face registers surprise. He hasn't noticed my approach.

'Oh. Hi, Dad.'

I long to hug and kiss him but know that he would rather I didn't. I quickly put my arm around his shoulders, squeeze, and remove it before he has time to object.

'Sorry to keep you. The train was late. Where shall we go?'

Letchworth on a midwinter weeknight at five-thirty

doesn't have much to offer. Pizza Hut or McDonald's.

'If you don't mind a ten-minute walk, Dad, we could try the golf club. Apparently they serve tea.'

'Sure. What time do you have to be back?'

'Eight at the latest.'

'I might try for the seven fifty-seven train if you don't mind. Otherwise it's the eight fifty-seven which doesn't get into London until after ten.'

I feel guilty because it will mean leaving him at seven-forty, depriving him of an additional twenty minutes we might have spent together. We squelch our way across the sports field.

'Dare I ask how Christmas was with your mum?'

'All right.'

'All right good, or all right bad?'

'Just all right.'

'Your younger brothers send their love. I've got some pictures they've done for you in my bag.'

Should I tell him now or later? It's probably more private outside, walking, than inside the golf club.

'Nat?'

'Yes, Dad.'

'Nat. I . . .'

He listens patiently.

'I, that is to say, Perrie and I, we . . . I . . . we have decided to . . . we are going to split up.'

No response.

I plough on. 'She is staying in Australia with Jack and Bert and I'm planning to travel backwards and forwards every few weeks.'

'Oh.'

'Are you upset?'

It takes him so long to answer that I am about to repeat my question when he blurts out, 'Not really. When will I see my brothers?'

'I hope you'll come out with me every holiday. When they are older Perrie might allow them to visit London.'

'But when will I see you?'

'I'll do what I've always done. When I am in London during the week I'll come up and take you out for tea or supper. We'll spend as many weekends together as I can manage. And there will be holidays. I've made sure I'll be around for your twelfth birthday.'

'Oh.' This time a small, choked, close-to-tears, desperate 'oh'.

'I am sorry, darling.'

The total inadequacy of my own parenting revolts me. I am failing this child but feel unable to do anything about it.

'Are you OK, Nat?'

'Yes.'

I know he doesn't want to be touched or comforted. I can't think what to say. We march on in search of refreshment. My bag is heavy. I have packed it with plenty of things to keep him amused over tea: quite a few presents, all carefully wrapped; also a games compendium, photographs of my Christmas in Australia, a choice of books to read out loud, his brothers' drawings.

In the middle of the night, barely awake, a three-year-old Bert braves the pitch black to come and find me. He navigates his way through the house, out of the back door, up the stairs, along the woodland path, on to the studio terrace, through the French windows and comes to rest at the bottom of the stepladder up to my sleeping platform.

'Who is it?' Disturbed by a strange noise, disorientated, I conclude that some wild beast has broken in.

'Me, Dad.'

'Bert?'

'Yes.'

'Oh, Bert!'

'I woke up and I missed you, Daddy.'

Whenever I leave for Europe Bert gives me a piece of satin edging from his blankie. I keep these tiny scraps of fabric in a wallet Nat has made for me and carry them with me everywhere.

'Hang on, I'll lift you up. Then we can have a cuddle.'

'. . . Then he let himself slide down until his legs were out of the rabbit hole, and dangled through the wall of the tunnel. "Here we go!" he said, and let himself drop. Whooooosh! He slid right into a dark, musty tunnel, and landed on soft earth. "Chuck me down a torch," he shouted. "It's pitch-dark in here. Did you remember to bring our torches, George?" Yes, George had four! "Look out!" she said. "Here comes one!" And she dropped it down the hole. She had already switched it on, so Dick saw it coming and caught it neatly. He shone it into the dark place around him. "Yes! It *is* a tunnel!" he shouted. "The secret passage, no doubt about it! I say – isn't this great? Come on down, all of you, let's share in the find together. Let's walk right up to the castle cellars. Come on, everybody! Come on!" End of chapter fifteen.'

'Go on, Dad. Don't stop there.'

'No. You've had five chapters, Jack. I think we'd better call it quits. More tomorrow if you like.'

'Oh, Dad. Pleeeeease.'

'Listen, it's long past your bedtime and I must go and get some breakfast. I'll ring tomorrow but you must remember to stay near the telephone after supper.'

'OK.'

'Night, night, darling. I love you and I miss you.'

'Yes. I miss you, too, Dad.'

'Sleep well, Jack.'

'Would you put the telephone down first, Dad?'

'All right. I love you. 'Bye. I love you.'

' 'Bye, D –'

I cut him off.

Perrie and I are sniping at each other in front of Nat. Upset, he goes and hides in his bedroom.

'Can we stop, please? It is distressing Nat.'

'Then you shouldn't have brought him.'

'Don't be ridiculous. He wants to see his brothers.'

'This isn't your house any more, Jonathan. You and Nat are here on sufferance. Remember, I decide whether you get to see the boys.'

We are in the kitchen. Livid, I slam a bottle of fizzy bitter lemon down on the counter and it explodes. Every surface, even the ceiling, is coated with fizzy bitter lemon. Perrie takes her car keys and goes out. Shaking with anger, I begin to clean up the mess. Nat comes down from his bedroom to help. I keep apologising to him. He keeps saying it is all right, not to worry. Afterwards I ask, 'Would you mind if, instead of going surfing, we went to look for a house to rent? I think we ought to move out.'

'Will Jack and Bert be allowed to stay with us?'

'Yes.'

'All the time I am here?'

'I think so.'

'Then let's go.'

When we have looked at half a dozen houses I ask him if he has a preference.

'No.'

'You really don't care?'

'No. As long as we can move into it quickly.'

Returning from the loo, where I've lingered because I'm bored, I glance into the drawing room and see the children belonging to the other lunch guests milling around, fed up. It occurs to me that this isn't their party, either. I'm there because I've been invited by a friend who does business with the host and, like the children, I'm waiting to be taken home. A boy of about seven, Jack's age, smiles at me. I get down on my hands and knees, make mooing noises, and scuttle in. It doesn't feel right, but I can't stop myself.

'Have any of you ever played ha-ha tummy?'

Grateful for a distraction, there are shy cries of no, what's ha-ha tummy, followed by much giggling.

'Well, line up in order of your size and we'll see if you lot can cut it.'

More giggling and with a bit of pushing and shoving they form a ragged line.

'Mmm. I said in order of your size. Here, you go here, and you go there. You're enormous, you should be at the end. How old are you? Ten? You're tall enough to pass for fifteen. And you look as if you are – let me guess – four. Only three? I was close.'

George's mother sticks her head around the door. 'Good heavens, I wondered where you had got to, Jonathan. We're about to serve coffee in the dining room if you'd like some.'

'I'm fine for a minute thank you, George's mother. Now all of you lift your shirts and pullovers so I can see your tummies. Stick them out as much as you can. You can stick them out more than that. Better. Good. Nine of the best tummies it has been my pleasure to inspect. Not quite as wobbly as I would have liked – you should try to eat more sweets. However, I think they'll do.'

George's mother is still watching.

'George's mother, are you in or out? In? Then let's have a look at your tummy. Call that a tummy? Push it out, woman. More. That's it. Now, I'll just test them.'

I work my way along the line, gently tickling each tummy in turn. The children laugh so much that they begin to fall over.

'You must have played this game before because I was about to ask you to lie down. On your backs. Is your tummy actually on your back and your bottom on your front? Come on, turn over. And be as quiet as you can. As quiet as eensy-teensy mices. Ssssh. You must be silent if the game is going to work.'

Nine little faces stare up at me expectantly. George's mother smiles doubtfully.

'Now, carefully as you can, put your head on someone

else's tummy so that it is like a pillow. Don't say anything. Just lie there quietly. Hush.'

Someone starts to giggle and their wobbly tummy sets off someone else. In seconds they are all in hysterics, their heads bobbing up and down, unable to contain their delight.

I suddenly recall Jack and Bert on the other side of the world and realise why this feels wrong. I shouldn't be amusing these children. Children I don't know, belonging to people I don't know. I should be with my own boys. I am overcome with remorse. This is adultery. I am being unfaithful to my own sons, repaying their loyalty with treachery. George's mother is speaking to me.

'I must ask, do you have children?'

'Yes and no,' I reply, but before I can explain what I mean we are joined by some other adults who want to play ha-ha tummy, too.

'Look what I've got, Dad.'

'What?'

Bert climbs on to my lap, his fist clenched tight.

'Be careful. They might escape.'

Slowly he opens his hand.

'What are they?'

'My seed family.'

In his palm are half a dozen orange seeds.

'Of course, silly me.'

'This is daddy seed. This is mummy seed. These are the

seed children. The seed children sometimes live with daddy seed and sometimes with mummy seed.'

Before I have time to say anything he becomes bored with the seed family, bored with sitting on my lap.

'Here, Dad, you look after them.'

Bert pushes the dysfunctional seed family into my hand and is gone. He appears to accept the new order and the only time he gets upset is when he has to go back to his mother's.

'I want to come with you.'

'I am afraid you can't.'

'But I want to. Why not.'

'Because Australia is your home now.'

'But I want to come to England and be with you and Nat. I'll ask Mummy.'

'I am sorry, darling, she'll agree with me.'

'You might stay in England.'

'I won't.'

'You might.'

Jack has been much more affected by the separation. His grief is pathetically apparent. Nervous and timid, overly enthusiastic to please, prone to prolonged attacks of depression, he tells me, 'I wish I was dead. I want to kill myself.'

At night he wets his bed, not once but twice and even three times. In the early hours of the morning I find him trying to change his sheets in the dark so as not to disturb me.

Jack refuses to talk about any of his feelings. When I try to tackle anything potentially sensitive with him he puts his fingers in his ears and repeats the words: 'I'd rather not talk about this, Dad. I'd rather not talk about this, Dad. I'd rather not talk about this, Dad.' Until I promise to change the subject.

I once ask him if he says the same thing to his mother when

she tries to discuss our break-up. He replies: 'I'd rather not talk about this, Dad.'

I understand completely.

'Well,' says yet another of my long-suffering and kindhearted friends, having listened patiently to me ranting on the subject of how much I miss my children, how badly Perrie has treated me and how fed up I am with travelling backwards and forwards to Australia, 'I think you are a terrific father and you shouldn't worry so much.'

Receiving praise for my parenting sickens me. I have denied my children a happy upbringing, perpetuated generations of misery. The last thing I am is a terrific father.

'Right! That does it. I am fucking fed up with you children. Absolutely fucking fed up. All you do is fucking squabble. On and on. It is doing my head in so . . . so I am going to do your heads in.'

Jack and Bert, who had been fighting with each other, suddenly stop. They focus on me, fear in their eyes.

'I have asked you repeatedly not to bicker. I ask politely. *And you fucking ignore me.*'

Infuriated, I reach out and knock their two heads together. Hard. I want it to hurt. Tears well up in their eyes. Aghast at what I have done, what I am doing, I find myself pushing and kicking them out of the kitchen.

'*Get out!* Get out of my sight. I don't fucking want to see you. Get into your bloody rooms.'

This happens, or a scene like it, at least weekly. Once I smack Bert so hard on his bottom that a red mark the shape of my hand is visible for several days. I am terrified that it will still be there when Perrie collects them. Every night I inspect it surreptitiously while he is having his bath, praying he won't bruise. I imagine being denied access to the children because I am violent.

I regret each outburst within seconds. In my shame I bang my head against the wall or bite myself or stab at myself with a knife.

'Just calling to let you know I landed safely. How are you?'

'I'm not sleeping well at the moment.'

'I am sorry, Jack.'

'I think it's my bed.'

'Could be.' Innocently: 'Do you find the bed in my house more comfortable?'

The bed. The choice of breakfast cereals. The help with homework. The holidays. The way the clothes are folded. The toys. The games we play. The trips we make. It is wrong, it is contemptible, but I want my children to tell me: 'You are a better parent than Mum is. We prefer being with you.'

Nothing is too much trouble if it'll prove my superiority. Jack's school lunchbox contains a four-course picnic including a linen napkin and handwipe. I get a toothpaste which is only available in America sent out to Australia by courier because Bert likes it. In my deranged state I am terrified that they will cease to be my children, that Perrie will take them over body and soul.

'What does a Polar Bear wear on his head, Dad?'

'Jack, is this from that wretched joke book I gave you?'

'Yeah.'

'Yes. Or yah. Not yeah.' I am on correctional autopilot. Perrie says ta, has dinner at midday, and calls the evening meal tea. She will definitely win the Vocabulary Battle though I still nurture absurd hopes of victory in the Field of Accent. It is ridiculous and even Jack knows it.

'Dad! Don't be such a snob. And the answer is: a polar cap.'

Perrie hints that our children don't love me as much as they love her. She says that, being boys, they will always love their mother more than they love their father. She says that when I am not there they never talk about me. She says that when they are grown up, when I can no longer control them as I attempted to control her before she broke free, they will rarely come to visit me, and then only out of a sense of duty. 'Look at your relationship with your own parents,' she says. 'Can you hope for anything better?' I don't suppose I can.

'Yes, yes, Johnny, I can quite understand that it must be tiring.'

'I'm exhausted, Dad. Completely worn out.'

'You know, I've been meaning to say to you: why not give

it a rest? Much as I enjoy you coming out so frequently, I think you should consider some other options.'

'What do you suggest?'

'Have you thought of just staying away for a year or two? Not coming to see them? Re-establishing your relationship when they are older and can appreciate you more?'

'Are you serious? I can't believe you are serious.'

'Quite serious. Look at the benefits. You'd save a great deal of money. Perrie would lose her primary bargaining chip. You'd have a chance to develop your career. And, if I may say so, the rest might help restore your temper.'

'There is no point in talking to you.'

'Dear boy. You don't want to become overly dependent on your children. Where will it leave you when they grow up? Mark my words, there comes a moment when children lose interest in their parents.'

'I think I just reached it.'

'If I may say so, you are very closed-minded. Well, well. We won't fall out about it.'

'Actually, we may. However, since we are speaking of your grandchildren, I was wondering if you would consent to visit them when I'm not here?'

'Drive over to see them, you mean?'

'Yes, that is what I mean.'

'It is an idea. I am afraid I couldn't do it regularly. I am far too busy. Not in the next few weeks, either. But later in the year, perhaps. I could take Sandra. Tell me, do you think Perrie might put us up?'

'Somehow, I don't.'

On the wall next to my desk, exactly six feet above the floor, where the plaster is soft, there is a small, circular, concave impression about seven inches across and an inch deep. Although it is smooth and polished at the centre of the impression, around the edges it has flaked and cracked. I am on the telephone to Perrie.

'I am sorry, Jonathan,' she says, 'you cannot speak with the boys today. It is not convenient.'

I stare at the shallow depression of plaster.

'And don't waste your breath telling me how much of an effort you are making. It is your choice. You don't have to come and see the boys.'

I can identify every single brush stroke the decorators have made – each minute ridge picked out in yellow paint.

'I don't think you have any idea how hard it is being a single mother.'

This strikes me as a bit thick, but I can't summon up sufficient energy to argue with her. I notice that a few of my hairs have become stuck to the plaster, that the general area is covered with greasy smudges from my forehead.

'Still, I am diverging from my main point which is that it isn't convenient for you to speak to the boys today. Goodbye.'

I replace the receiver, get up, and stand close to the wall, the tips of my toes just touching the skirting board. I slowly lean forward and fit my forehead into the hollow. I close my eyes and rest for a moment, my mind a blank. The plaster is cool and soothing. Gently I raise my head and smash it sharply down. A mild jarring of the neck. I do it again, this time considerably harder. A dull ache. And again, harder still.

'God, I am so stupid. I have made such a dreadful hash of everything. I apologise, Bert. I apologise, Jack. I apologise, Nat. I have really, really fucked up.'

Razor-sharp pain shoots through my skull, bright shapes dance in front of my eyes. I feel dizzy and nauseous. Satisfied, I take a step back and wait for my vision to clear.

I recognise the sound of Jack's bedroom door being opened and listen as he cautiously makes his way towards the kitchen. He keeps stopping and starting, obviously worried that he may not receive that warm a reception. I glance up at the clock, it is after ten. Earlier in the evening I lost my temper.

'Yes, Jack?'

I speak softly. He comes forward quickly, knowing from my voice that it is safe.

'I couldn't sleep, Dad.'

'Why not? It is terribly late, darling, and you have school tomorrow.'

'I am worried about money.'

I look at him closely and realise that he has been crying.

'Who isn't? Come and sit up on my lap. Now, how much have you got?'

'Twenty-three dollars. I'm not worried about that. How much do you earn, Dad?'

'Why do you ask?'

'Are you rich?'

'What a funny question.'

'Are you? Do you earn more than two hundred dollars a week?'

'Yes, I do.'

'Then you are rich.' His face desperately serious, full of concern for his mother. 'Mum isn't, you know. She is penniless. She told me.'

I fight to control my rage.

'Mum just feels poor. She has plenty of money, I promise you.'

'She doesn't.'

'Well, she has enough money to live in a lovely house and to drive a big car. She feeds and clothes you. You've got lots of toys. You take nice holidays. I expect she was joking when she said she was poor.'

'She wasn't. If you earn more than two hundred dollars a week you should give your money to Mum. You can afford it.'

I can't think how to answer him.

'If you won't give your money to Mum then I am going to get a job and she can have my wages so she won't be poor any more. I am also going to give her my twenty-three dollars.'

'Good heavens, Jonathan, what a lot of drugs you appear to be consuming.'

Will comes out of the bathroom clutching various containers.

'Put them back, please.' I don't like anyone touching my medication.

'What have we here?'

I reach to take them but he moves to avoid me and begins to read the labels. 'Mmm. Sleeping pills. Valium. Antidepressants. Beta-blockers. Antibiotics.'

I find myself blushing. 'They are to help with all the jet lag. And I've got some sort of chest infection, too.'

Will smiles knowingly. We are in the same boat now:

separated from our children; finding it difficult to come to terms with yet another new start; feeling raw.

'You poor bugger,' he says, throwing his arms around me.

I allow myself to cry.

'You baste it for twenty minutes . . .'

'A sort of chintz . . .'

'Oral, I tell you. There can't be any doubt . . .'

Mothers standing around the school entrance in small, animated groups exchanging news while they wait for classes to end. As I approach they lower their voices, lower their eyes and inch perceptibly away. It is a close-knit country town and I am an outcast. Perrie's much hated ex. The only man who collects his children. I hover uncertainly in the background longing for the bell to ring so that I can escape. The time passes slowly, each minute an eternity. Gradually the women relax and begin to forget I am there. The wife of an architect Perrie and I once employed accidentally meets my gaze and nods quickly.

I am relieved to get the boys back to the sanctuary of our rented house. I sit in the kitchen drinking tea and they romp around, summoning me as necessary.

'I'm finished! I'm finished!' Bert is calling.

As I squeeze into the cramped lavatory he leans forward to make it easier for me.

'Here's the paper, Dad.' He turns his head and looks up at me, his face puckered with concentration.

'Thanks.'

As I am helping him to get his trousers and underpants on he tries to wriggle free.

'Oi. Where are you going? Hands.'

'Oh, Dad.'

At the basin I have to adjust the water to precisely the correct temperature and then he uses so much soap that he can't wash it all off. I gently take his soft, slippery hands in mine and hold them under the tap.

'Will you play with me?'

Carefully I massage each finger, checking it for hidden deposits of soap.

'Will you play with me?

I stare hard at our interlocked hands, trying to imprint the image into my memory. Every moment with my children is of special significance. Even wiping Bert's bottom is so poignant that I can be moved to tears. He begins to pull away.

'Dad, will you play with me?'

At last I hear him. 'I must put supper on first. Afterwards. What shall we play?'

'Lego.'

'OK. Go and start. I won't be long. Here, dry your hands.'

He flicks water at me and runs off. While I am still mopping around the sink he comes back.

'Jack won't give me the Lego shark.'

'That's fair. You had the shark yesterday.'

'But I want it.' Bert pouts his lip in an expression I recognise as one of his mother's. He is trying to make himself cry.

'Let Jack have the shark. You can have it tomorrow.'

'No.'

Should I push it? Bert is the youngest and despite every effort to ensure parity, the reality is that he's somewhat spoilt. Jack doggedly polices the family with the purpose of hunting out partiality and preventing it (except when he's the recipient), but towards the end of the day the prospect of Bert having a tantrum can outweigh my sense of fair play. Bert continues to glower at me, much as his mother used to glower at me, and it seals his fate.

'Jack gets to keep the shark. Come and sit with me in the kitchen.'

'No.'

Bert stomps off to his bedroom to sulk. In the kitchen I boil water in the kettle for the pasta. A few minutes later I can hear Bert playing with his stuffed toys. He starts to sing.

Jack comes in. 'Here, Dad, I have done you a drawing.'

'Wow. That's great. Did you just do it?'

'Yes. It's the inside of a pymarid.'

'It's brilliant. I like all the detail.'

'This is the mummy.'

'Of course.'

'And this is a mummified cat.'

'Right.'

'Can I have a biscuit?'

'No. Supper is only ten minutes away.'

'You let Bert have a biscuit yesterday when supper was only ten minutes away.'

Of my three children, decisions handed down by the Parental Supreme Court are most likely to be challenged by Jack.

'I think you'll find you're wrong. No biscuits found their way into any little mouths before supper last night. Have a raw carrot.'

'I don't want a raw carrot.'

'It wants you. It's calling to you: "Eat me, Jack. Take me away from all of this."'

'Very funny, Dad.'

Jack stands as close to me as he can and watches everything I am doing. He sees me open the packet of tortellini.

'What's for supper?'

'Guess, brainy.'

'Pasta.'

'Right first time, You win a bis . . . What's the word? . . . a bisc-something. I know, a bisc – raw carrot.'

'Ho, ho, Dad. Highly amusing. Not.'

He takes a carrot and crunches it noisily with his mouth open.

'Off with you. Wash your hands and tell your brother to do the same.'

He drifts away and a few moments later fighting breaks out in Bert's room.

'Dad, he won't wash his hands.'

'Dad, Jack says I can't have any carrot.'

'You boys be nice to each other. Brothers must be nice to each other,' I shout back, but they aren't listening. Will and I frequently aren't terribly nice to each other, so I don't suppose my voice carries much conviction.

Later the three of us are tucked up in my bed with a pile of books. I have a cup of tea. They have little brown paper bags containing chopped apple and sultanas, just like my mother used to make.

'Here, you boys be careful of my tea.'

They have begun to bicker behind my back.

'Settle down, settle down. Anyone would think I had two exuberant boys on my hands. Which first? The telephone directory, the *A to Z* or the Shorter Oxford Dictionary?'

Bert thrusts *Doctor de Soto: The Story of a Mouse Dentist* into my hands.

'By William Steig,' I read, 'published by Arrow Books Limited. First published in the United States by Farrar Straus & Giroux Inc., New York. Copyright . . .'

Bert listens enthralled. He is being read his story and he is happy to hear every single word. Jack begins to twitch. 'Come on, Dad.'

I love reading to them in bed. We are safe. Nothing can touch us here. Bert will fall asleep while I am reading. But every day is too short for Jack. Even as a baby he couldn't bear the idea of falling asleep. When I finally close his book he snuggles up to me. 'One more chapter?'

'Nah.'

'Not nah, Dad. No, or since you have American blood, perhaps nope.'

'I lie corrected.'

We talk about grown-up subjects that you can't talk about when a boy aged three is listening in. I ask Jack his opinion on different matters. He tells me things he has learned at school; things that have happened. We whisper. Eventually I carry him into his bed, leaving Bert in mine.

Once they are both safely asleep I unlock the Evidence Cupboard and add Jack's drawing to the collection. On the back I write: Pymarid by Jack, 7. I enter fuller particulars in the Log. There are now more than a hundred exhibits in the cupboard: drawings, notes, photographs, and their gifts – shells, pebbles, toys, bits of Bert's blankie, even pieces of bark. Proof that my three boys really do care for me.

In the night Bert gets up and moves into Jack's bed. All the bedroom doors are open and in the morning I wake to the sound of Jack humming the theme tune from Bert's favourite television programme. He begins to tell a story using the same characters. I picture them cuddled up with each other, Bert's blue eyes staring lazily up at the ceiling as Jack entertains him.

During the last half-term holiday we went to a resort in Queensland. Nat couldn't come because his mother wanted him to do something else. He was philosophical. He doesn't like letting his mother down. On the first night I took the boys into early dinner with all the other children. Out of thirty parents attempting to feed their excited, over-tired kids, there were only two fathers: me, and a man with a sad face and two pretty daughters. Our eyes met and we acknowledged each other's presence but we didn't speak. In fact, we didn't speak all week. He was absorbed with his children. I was absorbed with mine. We watched one another, though. He was an extremely gentle man. All his movements were graceful. His daughters clung to him. He looked like a good father. I wondered, during that week, whether I looked like a good father. I wondered if I looked as sad as he looked. If we had been women in the same position we would have spoken. I wish I had opened a conversation. We might have become friends.

Jack finishes his story. Bert asks for more. Jack says no. Bert says OK. The two of them get out of bed and go to watch television. I lie in a foetal position thinking about the man with the daughters, about Perrie, about getting up and preparing breakfast.

'How have you been?' enquires my analyst.

I have been hitting my children. Boxing their ears. Beating them across their bottoms until my hand is so sore I sometimes think I have broken it. Cracking their heads together. Lifting them up bodily and shaking them. I am in despair about my behaviour. Once, when I appeared displeased and moved suddenly, they flinched, expecting to be struck. I notice that if I become irritated their faces register fear.

'Not bad, thank you. I am just back from Australia, of course.'

I am not in the least worried about doing them any serious harm. It would never come to that. But emotionally it must

213

be terrifying for them to see me snap. One minute calm and patient, the next roaring and crashing about.

'Did anything happen while you were there?'

I think I am having a nervous breakdown. I can't even tell any more if I am holding it all together or simply believe I am. Frequently, and for no discernible reason, I burst into tears. A couple of times I have become so overwhelmed that I just collapse on the ground wherever I happen to be. It upsets the boys. My devotion to them can't be called into question. They are always pleased when I pick them up and always miserable when I leave. Still, in my current state, how good a father can I actually be?

'Another court case over access visits and more wrangling about money.'

It is unseemly. Fighting the mother of my children. Attempting to defeat a woman who was once my closest friend.

'How did you respond?'

The night before the hearing I was so anxious I couldn't sleep. I sat up in the kitchen eating. Forcing more and more into my mouth in the ridiculous belief that it would soothe me. I started with muesli – became a muesli-eating machine – consuming bowl after bowl until a huge glass storage jar full was gone. Each heaped spoon represented a terrible, gut-wrenching sense of failure as a human being. An indescribable state of hopelessness and despondency. An urgent, insatiable need for some slight comfort no matter how ineffectual or damaging. Since Perrie and I have broken up my weight has ballooned from thirteen to over seventeen stone. I start a new diet every other day. In taking a single mouthful of cereal I am giving in, admitting that I cannot control myself, do not believe in myself.

'I found it a tad on the traumatic side.'

I moved on to the children's cereals – so-called 'fun' packs of Frosties, Crunchy Nut Cornflakes, Fruit Loops, Coco Pops – cereals I don't especially like. I ripped the lid off each cardboard box, mixing one with another, barely pausing to breathe. Still I wasn't sated. I found a packet of crackers – diet crackers – and the remains of a honeycomb. I used the crackers to scoop up great gobs of honey – cramming it into my mouth, washing it down with milk. Then I dozed on the sofa, upright because I felt so sick, until dawn.

'Go on.'

On the eighty-mile drive to Sydney for the court appearance I crashed my rental car and wrote it off. I had told the boys I would be home in time to collect them from school. Throughout the hearing all I could think about was that at ten past three the children would be outside the school gates and I wouldn't be there. In the end I got through to the school on a public telephone and a teacher looked after them for two hours. I was a wreck.

'Perrie won.'

Perrie is now in a position where, in theory, she can get a ruling barring me from any access to the children until they are eighteen. What she wants is for me to agree to her keeping all the money. It feels like blackmail but I am about to concede defeat. The fear of losing the children – the imperative of at least attempting to be a decent father to them – outweighs every other consideration.

'Where does that leave you?'

I have become that most repulsive of creatures: someone who sees themselves as a victim. I know I must move on but, unusually for me, I find myself without either the will or the energy to deal with my problems. I am so ashamed and unhappy I can't really talk about it.

'Beginning to worry about how I am going to manage.'

On top of everything else I am neglecting my marketing clients who, one by one, are taking their custom elsewhere.

A phantom child in the wardrobe, building a secret den

'It's me. Are the boys around?'

No reply, which means I am talking to Perrie.

'Please don't hang up. I have been trying to get through for days.'

I suspect her of screening every call in order to control when I do and don't speak with our children. A moment's tense silence followed by the sound of her retreating footsteps. Then, in the distance, she shouts out, 'Your father is on the telephone.'

From where I am sitting I look straight down on to South Anne Street, Dublin. At three o'clock in the morning it is surprisingly busy. In the murky half-light a stream of anonymous, shapeless figures flows in both directions. Occasionally a pedestrian steps under a street lamp and – for the briefest of instants – exposes himself to my scrutiny before plunging on into the darkness. Outside McGonigal's nightclub, opposite, a ragged queue of revellers waits patiently to gain admittance. The thump, thump, thump of electronic music is so penetrating that despite my double glazing I have to press my ear to the telephone in order to hear properly. Twelve thousand miles away it must be lunchtime. Without a word of explanation, Perrie replaces the receiver.

'Fuck.' I redial, stabbing at the buttons with such force that it hurts my finger.

'Could I have a word with the boys? Please.'

The line goes dead. On my third, fourth and fifth attempts I get the engaged tone. Furious, I bang the table with my fist. 'I don't believe it. The bitch.'

I have taken to holding entire conversations out loud with myself.

'There's no point in becoming indignant, Jonathan.' I speak soothingly, as to a child. 'You're tired and it's late. Leave it until tomorrow.'

'She knows I am desperate. She knows it.'

'My advice is calm down, get some rest.'

Reluctantly I fetch the futon from behind the filing cabinet. I have been living and working in the Dublin flat since our break-up because it is the only one of our properties held in my name. Anyway, it is so heavily remortgaged and I'm so behind on my repayments that I can't afford to move. What was the sitting room is now my office, the bedroom my secretary's office, the galley kitchen a storage area. Such sleeping as I manage takes place in the windowless hallway. As I make up a bed I chat away to myself.

'Don't dwell on it, mate. Concentrate on the task in hand. Where's the pillow got to? Here it is. Pesky thing. There, all done. Cosy. Convenient, too. Look at it this way: you have the shortest commute in the world. Pass me that bottle, would you? Thanks.'

I shake out some sleeping-pills – four or five yellow capsules of temazepam – and swallow them, uncounted, with water from the bathroom tap.

'That should knock you out, laddie.'

Wearily I get down on my hands and knees and crawl into bed.

'Not so much bedroom farce as hallway farce.' I laugh at the fact that there is insufficient space to stretch my legs.

'Always', I lie in the dark singing softly to myself, 'look on the bright side of life. Da dum, da dum, da dum.'

Four hours later I am up – showered, shaved, dressed and back at the telephone again.

'Hello?'

'Jack?'

'Hi, Dad.'

'How are you?'

'OK. We have just got out of the pool.'

'Will you ask Bert if he wants a few words with me?'

'Sure.' I listen as he attempts to persuade Bert to come to the telephone.

'Jack, don't worry. If he doesn't want to, don't make him. Jack?'

'Dad, I've tried but he won't.'

'Will you explain I love him?'

'Hold on,' then to Bert, 'Dad sends his love.' A muffled little voice calls out, 'I love him, too.'

'Any excitements, Jack?'

'Not really. Hang on. Yes, Mum? Mum says supper is on the table and I must go straightaway.'

'Oh. What a shame. I miss you and I love you.'

'Love you, too, Dad. Catch you later.'

And he is gone. I weep for a while. I have become the very thing I didn't want to be: an absent father.

I miss my children. Not in an abstract, intellectual way. Physically. I retch when I contemplate the enormous distance between us. I am consumed by vast, ill-defined fears for their safety and well-being. The thought of something dreadful happening to them, of not being there to protect them, makes me nauseous. Their removal from my daily life disorientates me, the line between reality and illusion has become blurred. Detached not just from my boys, but from the world itself, I exist in a trance-like state, struggling to make sense of what is happening around me. I suffer from separation-induced panic attacks in which I feel I am being crushed: a giant hand has caught me and is slowly tightening its grip, squeezing until I can no longer breathe.

They haunt me. Tall, gorgeous, blue-eyed, golden-haired boys. Walking to my favourite café for breakfast they race ahead of me; jumping, hopping, skipping along; darting in and out of the crowd; laughing and squabbling. Nat carries Bert across a road. Jack falls back to hold my hand. I reach down to embrace him and he vanishes, taking his brothers with him. At my desk I half turn and catch the three of them out of the corner of my eye, sitting quietly on the sofa reading. There's a child mirage under the table playing with toy cars. A phantom child in the wardrobe building a secret den.

Jack and Bert will be going to bed shortly. In my mind's eye I watch them getting ready. I see them flushed pink and wrinkly from their bath, wriggling into freshly laundered pyjamas, cleaning their teeth, having a wee. I imagine being there. Scooping them up, feeling their squirming ticklish bodies pressed against mine, gently dropping them on to their beds.

'You've left your teddy in the garden? Of course, I'll go and fetch him for you, wait a minute.'

I yearn to have their arms around my neck. Sense their sweet, warm breath upon my cheek as they kiss me good-night. Jack wants his back scratched. Bert runs his fingers through the remains of my hair.

What of Nat? He must be waking up right at this very moment. Last time I went to his school he showed me his dorm: a large, drab, gloomy room containing six identical beds, six identical chests of drawers, six identical desks, six identical chairs. It smelled strongly of feet. I picture him lying there, dozing, wishing he was somewhere else. The thought of him being cared for by strangers dismays me. The saddest part is his patient resignation.

'It's all right, Dad. I know you can't have me to live with you.'

'Hopefully things will settle down soon, darling.'

Perrie allows me to see as much as I want of his brothers but never lets me forget that she controls the access.

'Can't you force her to bring them back?' a colleague enquires.

'And have her hate me more than she does already? No thanks.'

We were so miserable together that I am secretly relieved she has left me. I could never have deserted the children. Better to be travelling 150,000 miles a year to see them than cohabiting with their mother. It is probably toughest on Nat, though, who comes out to Australia with me every school holiday. He only ever complains once, on a flight back to England. One minute he is describing some feature of his Game Boy, demonstrating how it works: 'Super Mario can leap in the air like this.' The next he falls slowly forward until his head touches my shoulder and he begins to sob. Noiselessly, barely moving. I pull him towards me and for the first time since he was small he lets me cuddle him. My shirt becomes wet with his tears, my arms turn numb, but still he doesn't stop. Finally, he pushes me away and accepts some tissues.

'I really miss my brothers.'

'I am sorry.'

'No. I really miss my brothers.'

'Oh, Nat, I am sorry.'

He regards me steadily for a moment and then goes back to his computer game. Perrie's latest proposals regarding visiting rights are that I should take Jack and Bert alternate weekends and half the holidays.

'It is absurd,' I rail, 'the travel is nearly killing me as it is.'

'Don't tell me. Tell your lawyer.'

221

She has already won an access battle over Christmas and is confident that in the future the court will be on her side.

'Mothers always know best,' the judge pronounced during the initial hearing.

I have become bitter and I hate myself for it. I don't want to be resentful or a whinger. It sickens me to hear myself condemning Perrie's actions while simultaneously justifying my own. I know perfectly well that I am equally responsible.

I complain about the injustice of the situation. 'Because she is a mother, she controls the children. Because everything we owned was held in her name, and the debt in mine, she controls all the assets.' Yet, in my soul I know I am guilty. Not just guilty of specific crimes against Perrie. Guilty of not being the sort of person I hold myself out to be. Guilty of not being good. All the dreadful things happening to me are a richly deserved punishment. I don't feel that I am terribly nice.

With family and friends I struggle to make light of the situation: 'So far as Perrie is concerned I have become the invisible man. She can't see me. She can't hear me. I am a *de facto* husband *non grata*'; 'Even my jet lag complains about having jet lag'; 'At least I am benefiting from plenty of sun. Anyway, how much worse can it get?'

But I am terrified that it could get considerably worse. Supposing Perrie succeeds in restricting my time with Jack and Bert? I have set myself the objective of being with the younger boys for a cumulative total of approximately six out of every twelve months. Supposing my health fails me? It is already deteriorating after only a year and if nothing changes I could be leading the same, transient lifestyle for a further fourteen years – which is when Bert turns eighteen. Supposing my income dries up? I am spending every penny I can earn, and borrowing heavily with the help of a dozen credit cards, in order to sustain the existing arrangements.

Supposing the kids reject me? They have every reason to be angry with a father who has let them down so badly.

When I am with my children I work hard to control my behaviour so that they see the positive side of my personality. I strive to hide the pain I feel as a result of our separation. It won't help them, after all, to witness their father crying, banging his head against the wall, mutilating his body. When we are apart I try not to let a day pass without letting them know that I am thinking of them. If only my parenting could be judged some other way – by the hours I have spent reading stories on to cassette tape for each of my boys, or the number of parcels containing comics and sweets I have posted, or my annual output of faxes, or the size of my telephone bills.

Either he observes the rules or he doesn't play at all

That I would have to endure so much more of my father's company was an unforeseen side-effect of my relationship with Perrie. It had not occurred to me that having an Australian partner would lead to numerous holidays (let alone property ownership) in the same locality as a man I would otherwise have sought to avoid. A sporadic correspondence and infrequent meetings suddenly metamorphosed into regular contact. While Perrie and I were a couple, while Sandra was still alive, this was unpleasant but not unbearable. The women kept the more irascible side of my father's personality in check. He picked fights with us all but there was safety in numbers and we worked as a team to maintain a relatively peaceful environment. Having children around also eased the situation.

When my father said, 'I want to see a little of my grandchildren,' that is precisely what he meant. He desired proximity without engagement and was delighted to have them in his general environs, providing it didn't mean altering his routine.

'I understand that they have to go to bed early. But does this mean we all have to eat dinner at six? Surely seven-thirty would be soon enough?'

'Really, Dad, it has to be six.'

'Ridiculous. Seven, and not a minute sooner.'

Concessions were made if something he wanted to do anyhow could be adapted to something which would amuse the children, or vice versa. For instance, he was perfectly content for us all to go to the skateboard park Nat liked because it was next to a nature reserve where he could walk the dog. In fact, all outdoor activities met with his total approval, as did visiting any type of museum. What he couldn't abide was popular entertainment. Nothing on earth would have induced him to watch a children's movie, enter a theme park or go shopping. Dutifully, he would take his grandchildren to a toy shop once a year and allow them to pick out a combined birthday and Christmas present. Otherwise he would not so much as enter a newsagent's in order to buy them a comic.

Though contact with his grandchildren was on his terms, it was affectionate. He would willingly have looked after them by himself had he not been deemed too absent-minded by their mothers and me. As a small baby Nat sustained severe bruising when Grandad dropped him in order to shake someone's hand at a party. As a toddler Jack was abandoned in a playground when Grandad forgot about him and came home alone. In short, supervised bursts he told them stories, played board games with them or taught them golf. With regard to the latter, he demonstrated a remarkable tolerance by allowing very small boys indeed to practise their driving in his back garden.

It wasn't that my father didn't get upset when Perrie left me and returned to live in Australia: 'What a shame. I am sorry. Horrible for you to go through. Poor darling.' But within our family the ending of a relationship bordered on being an everyday occurrence. Pity and understanding were meted out to the victim, the practicalities discussed, enquiries into the state of the separation made. It was not, however, treated as being anything more than a temporary setback. Furthermore, although he worried about my health and the stress it put me under, one aspect of the new arrangement suited him admirably: 'The silver lining, dear boy, is that I get to see you every few weeks.'

His enthusiasm for my company increased dramatically after Sandra unexpectedly fell ill and died. I never saw him as badly shaken by a death as I did at the loss of Sandra. He regretted the passing of friends and relatives in England, whereas he mourned for Sandra.

'Ah, Johnny, I was ringing to say I could come to you on the twelfth for about a week.'

What brought pleasure to my father was a harrowing obligation for me. My overall philosophy was to avoid him as much as possible without causing offence. When he suggested dates for getting together in England I could pretend to be going abroad, or to have pressing business engagements. In Australia he knew that my sole commitment was to Jack and Bert, and this made it hard to come up with plausible excuses as to why we shouldn't meet.

'You know, Dad, I think I might bring the boys up to you.'

Given the inevitability of seeing him, I found it easier to drive up to Canberra, where he lived, than to have him staying with us. An enthusiastic guest, once he had made the four-hour journey to the coast he was inclined to stop for considerably longer than I would have chosen. Having him in the house disturbed my finely balanced routine; it substantially reduced the amount of time I had available to look after my boys; and it made work impossible. He expected me to entertain him, and though he conversed briefly with his grandchildren, they were largely ignored. It infuriated me how he could have the energy for a long walk and a round of golf, but then claim to be too tired to play with Bert for more than ten minutes.

'Oh, I was looking forward to a few days by the sea. Still, if you prefer it the other way around. You will come for the week?'

'Of course we will.'

I lied. The main benefit of taking the boys up to Canberra was that I determined the length of our visits. Instead of seven days of Grandad I could escape with a long weekend or, during term, just a Saturday and Sunday. I had also established the principle that we stayed in a hotel, rather than at his house, which meant I only had to endure him until around eight in the evening when I put the boys to bed.

I avoided my father in order to protect myself. He never distressed me more than after my separation from Perrie. I was in an especially vulnerable condition and without her there was no third party to act as a buffer between us. It got to the stage where I could barely stand his presence. Meals were a nightmare. Instead of a table and chairs in the kitchen he had a booth arrangement that required us to squeeze up close to each other on benches. I would sit in agony watching (and listening to) him eat with his mouth open – nauseated by the tiny particles of food which came flying out as he spoke.

Of course, the real issue was what he said. As he got older he became more belligerent and intolerant than he had ever been before. He contradicted me on principle and most conversations – no matter how innocuous the topic – swiftly became acrimonious. A classic example of this was when my father began shouting at me because I had corrected him regarding the year of Nat's birth.

'Listen, Johnny. I'll spell it out for you again in words of one syllable. Your son was definitely born in 1983. Will you pay attention? 1983. Not 1982. Not 1984. But 1983!'

We were in the dining room in Canberra. Jack and Bert sat in silence, used to Grandad's outbursts. I tried to explain, without becoming angry, why I knew that Nat had been born in 1982. I couldn't bear to lose my temper in these confrontations with my father and would eventually back down rather than show my irritation.

'Fine, Dad, have it your own way. Nathaniel was born in 1983.'

Once, and only once as far as I can recall, did I become really upset with him. He was showing Bert how to play chess. Bert was moving out of turn and this irked my father who began to raise his voice. 'Bert, will you play properly? I have told you already you can't move your bishop in that direction. Anyway, it isn't your go. It is my go.'

Seeing Bert's face begin to crumple, I intervened. 'Dad, all Bert wants to do is have a game of chess with his grandfather in the same way that his brothers do. Just let him move the pieces around the board and don't worry about it. He is only five.'

'Either he observes the rules, or he doesn't play at all.'

'Dad, it is a game and he is only five.'

'It doesn't matter. The fun in playing is to win. You can't win if you don't observe the rules. He is not observing the rules, so I won't play with him.'

I lost control. 'He is only five, Dad. How can I get that into your thick skull? Five, five, five. A small boy of five who just wants to sit with his grandad and have a little fun . . .' I began to cry with frustration. Then I screamed at him: 'For heaven's sake, go easy on him, he is only five.'

'The boy plays properly, or not at all. That's final.'

Bert crept from the room. I started to hurl abuse at my father, who slowly and deliberately got up and left the room himself. 'You selfish bastard. All you can ever fucking think about is yourself. I can't believe that you want to win a game of chess with a five-year-old. It is pathetic. You are pathetic.'

'I shall have a cigarette in the garden while you compose yourself, Jonathan. I do not have to take this from you. You are over-excitable. I blame your mother.'

Later I apologised because it seemed the easiest thing to do.

Lingering over the remains

The tide is out and the sand is as flat and hard as a pavement.
I have walked the length of the beach, my eyes fixed on the
surf in the hope of seeing a dolphin. Schools of fish swim in
the giant breakers, flashing silver as the light catches their
scales. Seven in the morning and it is already extremely
warm. I clamber across some boulders, paddle through a rock
pool, and scramble up the path to the top of the cliff. The
view is breathtaking. A rugged, green coastline interspersed
with smooth, golden beaches, a vast plain of meadows and
forests set against a spectacular backdrop of hazy blue moun-
tains. All basking in the sun, clean and bright and fresh, the
colours rich and vibrant.

'Can you receive me, Baldy? Over.'

'Baldy to Little Squirt. So you are up, are you?'

Worried about leaving the boys home alone while I take my
early morning walk, we stay in contact using walkie-talkies.

'Can I play the Nintendo?'

'Is Nat up, Bert?'

Nat sleeps on a makeshift bed in the same room as the television. He is visiting for a week over his half-term holidays.
The first time in several months we have all been together.

'I'll see.'

'No, Bert, you'll wake him.'

Too late.

'He's up now, Dad. Smell you later. Over and out.'

Nat and I have just arrived from London and in the excitement none of us went to bed much before one in the morning. Yet Bert is up and bouncing with energy only six hours later. It used to be that when he came to stay with me after a period apart there was a certain shyness between us. I felt I had to woo him, win him over, prove my place in his affections. I suspect his diffidence was born of self-preservation. When all the madness started he was too young to understand that I wasn't abandoning him: that I would be back. Now the transition between his mother's world and my own doesn't appear to bother him.

'Calling Baldy. Calling Baldy. Do you copy?'

'Yes, Bert?'

'Can we take the go-cart out into the street?'

'No. You'll wake the neighbours.'

'OK. See ya.'

Bert is by far the most energetic of my sons. He is a runner and a jumper and a climber. It is Bert who bullies his brothers and me into playing football and cricket, who instigates bike races and tennis matches, who begs to be taken to the local swimming pool and skating rink. He has forced me to become a different sort of a dad – more active, more athletic.

'Helmut Lang's women's collection is nowhere near as user-friendly as his menswear.'

'I quite like that evening gown.'

When I get back Nat and Jack are sitting at the kitchen table poring over a glossy magazine.

'What on earth are you looking at?'

'*Vogue*,' explains Nat, 'I bought it by mistake at the airport.'

'It is more interesting than you would imagine,' says Jack, who has an insatiable curiosity. He hungers after knowledge and his conversation is peppered with facts and figures, speculations and theories.

'The word "fashion" comes from the Latin, *factionem*, which means to make. I looked it up. In the encyclopedia I noticed that the earliest reference to fashion was . . .'

When he is in full flow we tease him by saying that we are tuned to 'Radio Jack'. He is fascinated by words and has developed an impressive vocabulary. During a tennis lesson – aged seven or eight – he wanted to know what velocity the ball was travelling at and when his coach couldn't answer Jack enquired witheringly if, at least, he knew its trajectory.

'You've just got to hit it, Jack.'

Jack wasn't attracted by anything so prosaic. He has the physique and coordination to be good at sport – he is the fastest swimmer in his class – but he isn't in the slightest bit competitive. Perrie once asked him if he wouldn't like to win a particular swimming award and he replied: 'Why?'

Panache is not a word that one would normally apply to a boy. Yet from a young age Jack demonstrated an abnormally individualistic style. His thought processes and habits might be considered mildly eccentric in an adult; but in a child they set him apart from his contemporaries. A taste for luxury and idleness has earned him the nickname Noel, after Noel Coward. Sporting pyjamas, a monogrammed dressing-gown and a cravat, he has been known to pass whole days stretched out on my large, velvet sofa staring ruminatively at the ceiling. Forced to give a three minute 'show and tell' type speech at school, the subject he selected for his discourse was not, as his teacher had suggested, 'my pet' or 'my favourite toy' but 'ethics'. One summer holiday he taught himself a Latin quotation each day.

'Go on, off with you both, and I'll make breakfast.'

I like our meals to be an event. While the three brothers bond in the other room over the Nintendo, I squeeze fresh juice, lay the table and start to make French toast. I confine myself to fruit for breakfast. I have been eating sensibly and exercising regularly with the result that my weight has almost returned to normal. I've cut out bingeing. It requires immense effort and constant vigilance but being able to control my body, when there is so much in my life that I can't control, has vastly improved my overall state of mind. I still suffer from intermittent mood swings, but I can honestly say that I am not depressed. In fact, I would go so far as to describe myself as content, occasionally even joyful.

'Bert, don't do that.' Nat sounding annoyed.

Bert needs to be the centre of attention and if he is ignored for too long can be relied upon to remedy the situation. I have seen him launch unprovoked attacks on both his siblings for no conceivable reason other than the desire for a reaction. As the youngest he feels confident that someone will look after and protect him. If things aren't going his way he knows that his appearance will stand him in good stead – it is difficult to resist his angelic, tear-stained face. Bert is quite capable of crying on my shoulder while simultaneously doing a 'rude sign' behind his back at his brothers. Nat laughs at his antics and calls him a rascal and a scamp, but Jack, since he is closer in age, finds Bert infuriating.

'I hate you, Bert,' Jack screams and there is a thump as something hits the wall.

I don't know how to respond. I want my children to get on better than my brothers and me. It occurs to me that inadvertently I have duplicated the exact circumstances of my own upbringing. Nat, Jack and Bert are juxtaposed in the same pattern as Nick, Will and me: two younger brothers, close in age, with a considerably older half-brother living overseas. Wallowing in self-pity, obsessed by the thought that my children had been denied a permanent father, I was slow to recognise that for them the hardest part of what has happened may be the loss of each other. When they grow up they will share me, but they won't share much of a common past.

The sense of displacement is likely to be greater for Jack and Bert (as it was for Will and me) than for Nat. Having separated parents of different nationalities, one of whom also came from separated parents of different nationalities, is bound to leave them somewhat rootless and unsettled. I can't help wondering where we will all end up. My hope is that one day we might live in or near the same city. My fear is that we will never have a proper centre to our lives; that no matter what I try to do to anchor us we are doomed to drift slowly away from each other: Nat in one country, Jack in a second, Bert in a third, and me in a fourth. For this reason, while they are still young, I consider it imperative that the boys spend every possible moment with one another.

'Do stop fighting,' I shout, 'breakfast is ready.'

In they bounce, Jack giving Bert a piggyback, Nat bringing up the rear, the quarrel evidently over. I quiz them on what they would like to do for the day.

'Stay home,' says Jack, who hates going anywhere.

'A theme park. Maybe Wonderland?' Bert suggests optimistically, knowing full well it would mean four hours of driving.

'Whatever.' Nat is the easiest-going of the boys.

Earnest negotiations follow and eventually it is agreed that we'll take a picnic lunch and climb through rainforest to a local waterfall.

'That sucks.' Bert still clinging to the idea of Wonderland.

'Anyway,' I point out, 'we can't go to Wonderland today because Mum is coming this morning to see your new rooms.'

After several years of dilapidated, temporary, rented accommodation I have managed to buy a small house for us to live in. There isn't a bedroom for Nat and there aren't any proper reception rooms but it is jolly and it is ours. There is a decent-sized garden, too, and at night we fall asleep to the sound of the ocean. As soon as we took possession Bert – seemingly oblivious to the tension between his parents – asked: 'Could you invite Mum over to see my room?'

My relationship with Perrie is frosty. Long ago I relinquished any expectation of her returning even a modest amount of money to me, let alone agreeing to an equitable financial settlement. She has stopped threatening to restrict my access visits. I'd be lying if I said I had managed to purge myself of all resentment towards her. Still, the relief of our not being in perpetual conflict outweighs any lingering sense of injustice. We both love our children and want what is best for them. In this, at least, we are united. Telephoning her to make arrangements for a visit she said, 'All right. I will drop in quickly on my way up to Sydney.'

Perrie is away most of the week, working. When I am not there the boys are left with a housekeeper. Even at home their mother is extraordinarily industrious, taking in paying guests and running an Internet company. Ironically, she has become driven, the very thing she hated about me. I, on the other hand, have given up the idea of a career. The travel made it impossible to carry on in marketing or to maintain any business interests. Instead, I have moved into publishing. I work in intense bursts when not caring for the boys and am rather pleased to be free of gibes about being a junk-mail writer.

As promised, Perrie only stays briefly and we are able to set off on our expedition before the day becomes unbearably hot.

'Mum is sexing David.'

'It isn't sexing, Bert, it is having sex with.'

Nat and I are accidental eavesdroppers. Jack and Bert chattering away in the back of the car unwittingly answering questions about their mother's life I would never dream of asking them, although, of course, I am curious. Perrie only addresses me when it is unavoidable. If she needs to convey information she does so through her solicitor or sends me a fax: 'Jack has a dentist's appointment at 2 p.m. Thursday'; 'Bert needs the following items of school uniform.'

She is much more assured as a mother than I am as a father. I am forever soliciting the boys' opinions on aspects of my parenting: 'Do you think I should allow you to stay up this late on a school night? Does Mum let you play over an hour a day on the computer? Have I become a nag?'

I have apologised for how I behaved towards them during and after the break up with Perrie. I've tried to explain it and to encourage them to direct their own anger in a more appropriate manner. It is an accepted part of our family lore that there was a period when Dad was always cross and smacking them, that it was wrong of me. Sweetly, they tell me to forget it. I reply: 'I won't stop worrying until you are grown up, happy and forming healthy relationships.'

At least I have been able to alter my conduct. I never lift a hand to them now and have no trouble keeping my temper in check. I have become almost too patient. When I recently growled at Jack, 'I'm going to get jolly annoyed if you don't do as I request,' he replied, with absolute certainty, 'No, you won't.'

Not hitting the children. Not mutilating myself. Not being dependent on, or addicted to, anything. Not working at something I deplore. These are the tangible benefits of several years of therapy. I make fun of it: 'Thanks to shrinkage I am virtually cured.' Whereas, in truth, I attribute my increasing self-awareness to analysis. I was a slow starter, unable to see the benefit of talking about my problems. Without therapy, however, I doubt I would have been able to instigate change in my life, let alone achieve some measure of peace.

'Sexing David, having sex with David,' says Bert, 'who cares?'

'Anyway, she isn't. Just because they were sleeping in the same bed doesn't mean they were having sex,' Jack retorts hotly. 'You don't have sex with your teddy.'

A pause. Jack leans conspiratorially over the driver's seat: 'Dad?'

'Yes?' I reply cautiously, steeling myself for a query about the facts of life.

'Can we listen to a tape?'

We listen to a lot of tapes in the car. I record dozens of programmes from Radio Four in England and bring them out with me.

'Why don't we play our own version of *Just a Minute*?' I suggest. 'Nat can set the subject and be the judge since he has a watch with a timer.'

'I'll go first,' insists Jack, 'what is my subject?'

'Why I love Gemma Nichols.'

This is a reference to Jack's girlfriend.

'At least I've got a girlfriend,' points out Jack, 'unlike any of the other men in this family.'

'Not true,' pipes up Bert, 'Grandad has a girlfriend.'

'Several,' whispers Nat under his breath.

'I heard that, Nat,' says Jack.

Grandad's girlfriends are a source of untold fascination to the boys. They giggle when he introduces even the slightest of female acquaintances, afterwards speculating on whether she might be one of his 'special friends'. In an unwise moment he admitted to passing afternoons on the sofa in his office 'canoodling with a valued work colleague'.

'What', enquired Jack subsequently, 'is canoodling?'

'Don't go there,' advised Nat.

We reach the bottom of the trail to the waterfall. Bert is persuaded, reluctantly, to leave his Game Boy in the car. Jack delays us for five minutes searching for a suitable walking stick. Nat refuses to wear a hat because it looks silly. Once we get going Jack and Bert charge ahead, Nat dropping behind to keep me company.

'Dad, will you help me with my revision when we get back?'

'Of course.'

Although academic work is a struggle for him, he perseveres.

My decision to maintain such close contact with his brothers has meant I have had less time for Nat, which is an acknowledged source of sadness to both of us. Despite this, we have a strong relationship. Though we don't see as much of each other as we would wish, we speak almost every day – often twice. He is tall, like me; good looking, like his mother, but seems oblivious to how handsome he is. Waiting for him once outside his school I overheard two girls: 'Nat is cool.' 'Yeah.'

Nat has a dry, slightly mocking, self-deprecating sense of humour. He delivers witty and sophisticated one-liners with a deadpan, almost apologetic look on his face. 'For a dyspraxic such as myself to accompany you skiing', he explained at age eleven, 'would be the sporting equivalent of me putting my head in a gas oven.'

He has overcome many of the physical and learning difficulties he had before he went to boarding school. There's a surprising boldness to him, too. Recently he showed me how he was able to get into the private frequent flyer lounges at Heathrow. 'It is all a matter of smiling and looking purposeful, Dad.'

His younger half-brothers absolutely worship him and he is ever mindful of their needs. 'If you were going to read my history book to me, Jack could do worse than listen in,' he suggests as we make our ascent through the rainforest, 'it might be useful to him in the future.'

We come across Jack and Bert sprawled on the ground. At our approach they leap up and bound on ahead.

'Last one up stinks,' shouts Berts over his shoulder.

Nat and I struggle after them. When we reach the waterfall they are hanging around nonchalantly, whistling through their teeth. We sit down to the picnic, Bert flopped over my legs, Nat and Jack leaning against a fallen tree.

'This is heaven,' says Nat, echoing my own thoughts.

My sons are at ease with each other. There is a fair amount of rough and tumble, a great deal of friendly teasing and banter.

'Jack, your ears do stick out a hell of a way,' remarks Nat conversationally as he munches on a sandwich.

'No, Nat, I am just straining to hear.'

Jack declined an operation to pin his ears back on the grounds that it might affect his ability to wiggle them. All the boys can wiggle their ears.

'Nat, your ears stick out as well,' says Bert, standing up for Jack, 'and your feet smell.'

'Your bottom smells,' chorus Nat and Jack in unison, falling about in laughter as Bert blushes.

After returning from the waterfall we pass the remainder of the afternoon seated around the kitchen table, each engaged in a different activity. I read aloud from Nat's history book and he makes notes. Bert manufactures tiny plates of ham and eggs from clay. Jack produces 'highly detailed working drawings of vehicles suitable for the exploration of the Earth's moon'. Bert suddenly springs to his feet, announces that he could now feed breakfast to eleven miniature soldiers, and disappears to play on the computer. Taking his lead, Nat and Jack follow.

'Supper in half an hour,' I call after their retreating forms.

I prolong each stage of the evening to make it last. Supper, unlike breakfast or lunch, occupies the best part of an hour. We linger over the remains of the meal, chatting and playing word games. Bert hangs off me. He is a tremendously tactile boy. I am astounded when any of my children voluntarily make bodily contact. I ask if they would like to watch television while I clear the table and load the dishwasher.

'We'll tidy. You cooked.'

I shoo them away. It is a pleasure to do things for them. The chores completed, I carry first Bert and then Jack upstairs for a shower. Nat tags along. Afterwards we gather in my bedroom. There's a pillow fight during which a light gets broken. We play tiddlywinks, snap and dominoes. I read a chapter of John Buchan for Jack and a chapter of Richmal Crompton for Bert. Nat goes downstairs and cuts up some apples and everyone has a late night snack. I tuck Bert in. As I go to kiss him he throws his arms around my neck and refuses to let go.

'Dad?'

'Yes, my little angel?'

'Nothing.'

'Come on, shut your eyes.'

'Dad?'

'What is it?'

'Nothing.'

I sit with him until he drops off to sleep. Next to Jack's room, where I find him reading something he has written to Nat. Jack's favourite hobby is writing. I join them. We hold a whispered conversation about what we might do tomorrow. Nat and I kiss Jack goodnight and head downstairs to watch a film. Five minutes pass and Bert appears, wanting a glass of water. A further five minutes and Jack appears claiming to have a strange pain in his knee. In fact, at frequent intervals for the next hour, one or other of them interrupts us demanding hugs, something extra to nibble on, another few pages of their book, a little chat, an opportunity to see a bit of the movie. My it-really-is-time-for-you-to-go-to-sleep is half-hearted. Nat is sixteen, Jack eleven, Bert seven. They are growing up and I want to hold on to every glorious moment of their childhood while I can.

I was hoping for a better death than this

My father sat slumped in the passenger seat of his car – an elderly and rusty Ford Cortina – outside the accident and emergency entrance to Woden Hospital. He was wearing a string vest, a grubby pair of purple pyjamas, a stained mackintosh several sizes too small for him, and black leather shoes without socks. On his head he had an ancient tweed cap which had belonged to his father, and in his arms he clutched a battered briefcase containing notes for his memoirs, spare handkerchiefs and a Billy Bunter book.

The car was parked in direct sunlight and its interior was like an oven. My father was perspiring profusely. Next to him, in the driving seat, his stepdaughter Karin wilted patiently.

The automatic glass doors of the hospital whooshed open and a small party of white-coated emissaries – blinking furiously in the sudden glare – cautiously approached the car to discuss terms. My father became animated, shouting his conditions through the window. The white-coated emissaries listened and withdrew to consider their position further.

'I am not', he repeatedly bellowed at Karin, 'going in there until they assure me I won't be in the ward your mother died in. Your mother was killed by the incompetence of the doctors on that ward and I don't intend to go the same way.'

They waited. People came and went from the hospital. No one paid any attention to the car. After an interminable period an orderly pushing a wheelchair was disgorged by the whooshing doors.

'Professor Self? I am to take you up to your bed.'

'What is he saying?' My father grimaced as he fiddled with his hearing aid.

'He says he is here to take you up to your bed,' relayed Karin.

'Yes, but the point is, which ward is the bed in? Ask him that.'

Karin turned to the orderly, who shrugged.

'He doesn't know.'

'Well, we stay here until he does know. Tell him to go back and find out which ward, and tell him to hurry. I need a pee.'

Following several days of prevarication, negotiation and postponement my father begrudgingly admitted himself to hospital for tests. It was his first ever stay in a hospital. He was nearly eighty.

Only too grateful to have been in transit from England while my father debated whether his symptoms warranted hospitalisation, I went to see him the morning after I landed. I was more concerned, as I drove up to Canberra, about the arrangements I had put in place for Jack and Bert to be collected from school than I was about my father's medical condition. I always thought of him as a passive hypochondriac – happy to hypothesise that (and behave as if) his indigestion was a heart attack or his need for stronger prescription glasses the onset of blindness – but without sufficient will to become unwell. When I had last seen him, just before Christmas, he had been as fit and active as ever – working, walking, gardening and socialising with the energy of a man in his twenties. Indeed, during that particular visit one of his three mistresses had explained to me in awestruck tones that: 'your father is physically vigorous – amazingly vigorous – very, very, very vigorous'. It occurred to me at the

241

time that his body, somehow aware of his arrested emotional development, was politely trying its best to remain youthful.

He was asleep in a chair when I arrived, snoring, his head slumped forwards. I perched on the bed as quietly as I could but he woke up immediately with a start.

'Ah, there you are, Johnny. I am glad you have got here.'

I leaned over and kissed him. He made a feeble attempt to embrace me. He smelled of disinfectant.

'It is good of you to come.'

Our eyes met for an instant and then he began to fall asleep again. With an effort he forced himself awake. 'Good of you to come,' he repeated in a distant voice. He lifted his arm and waved it in a vague gesture of explanation. 'I was writing a few letters. It has been a tiresome day. Tests, you know. Lots of ruddy visitors. Not you, dear boy. From the church, mostly. And a few from the university.'

The thought of the visitors seemed to jerk him awake. He became animated.

'Have you had any lunch? No? I believe you can get quite a decent sandwich in the cafeteria. You can go down in a moment while the nurses are attending to me.'

'What do the doctors say, Dad?'

'Doctors? Don't talk to me about doctors. First it is one thing, then it is something else. My legs have swollen up. My chest hurts. I feel weak. I get these incredible fevers every few hours. And I am having terrible trouble swallowing. They put me on a new drug for my blood pressure last month and it could all be a side-effect of that. Thrombosis? No one knows. My liver is enlarged. It has been suggested, *en passant*,' he paused for the briefest of moments, 'that I may have cancer, but they aren't saying much on the subject. Anyway, I feel much better now you are here. Who did you fly with?'

'KLM.'

Cancer.

'Decent flight?'

It had never occurred to me that he might get cancer. It seemed far too modern a disease for him. Too fast. Too popularist. I had it firmly implanted in my mind that he would suffer a long series of mild strokes: 'How is your father?' 'He has had another stroke, I am afraid, though it hasn't affected him badly.' I was under no illusions regarding his mortality, but I saw him gradually slowing down – doing a little less each year, cutting back to just the one mistress, eventually moving into a nursing home, finally a call from matron telling me that he had died in his sleep. I was so certain of this future that I had begun to wonder whether I shouldn't start to budget early for his nursing-home fees.

'Any flight that lands is decent enough so far as I am concerned, Dad.'

Cancer. Cancer. Cancer. As I repeated the word to myself I realised that I desperately wanted it to be cancer. Serious, incurable, inoperable, untreatable, fatal cancer.

'I suppose you had to come via Amsterdam.'

'Yes. When will you hear about the test results?'

Irritably: 'I don't know. The whole thing is sinister in my opinion. Don't you consider it sinister?'

As a child I had longed for him to die. I had no desire to see him suffer, I just yearned for him to be dead. I had spent hours fantasising about how much better life would be without him. Now, in the fraction of time it took to utter the single word 'cancer', those dreams had been resurrected. I searched his face hoping to find a clue as to the seriousness of his condition, a sign that this wasn't a false alarm, that death was close. I searched in vain. He looked tired and he looked cross but he didn't look as if he was about to die. Feeling a rush of empathy towards him, I stayed much longer than I meant to.

I visited him in hospital two days later, and again two days after that. Before the fourth visit Karin telephoned with the prognosis.

'Bad news, I am afraid. Cancer of the liver and there is nothing they can do. His doctors say he is unlikely to live more than a few months.'

'Can't they be more precise?'

'No. Not without a biopsy and he refuses to have one.'

'Why?'

'He can't see the point.'

'But with a biopsy they would have a better idea of . . . ?'

'Yes.'

For a moment I couldn't stop myself from thinking how typically selfish it was of my father. I wanted to know how long I would have to pace myself.

'How is he taking it?'

'Hard to say.'

'I'll come tomorrow.'

'He's going home tomorrow. Why don't you leave it a day?'

I went every second or third day after that – dropping Bert at school early in order that I could get to Canberra before lunch, leaving by tea so that I was back at the coast in time to tuck both boys into bed – determined that attending to my father should have the least possible impact on my children. The round trip involved seven hours of hard driving. I stopped for half an hour each way in Goulbourn – a dusty, moribund town built around a prison – and took tea in the Paragon Café to calm myself down. That huge, old-fashioned, sombre restaurant with its huge, old-fashioned, sombre waitresses served as a perfect counterbalance to my mood – for I found those journeys strangely invigorating, even exhilarating. I revelled in their sense of purpose, their rhythm, their isolation. I drove too fast and too recklessly for safety.

On the first occasion I saw my father after he returned

home from the hospital he greeted me with the words: 'You've heard the news, dear boy?'

'Yes, Dad. I am sorry.'

'I'm not sure how I'll manage.'

'That's all right, Dad, I'll look after everything.'

'Good. I hoped you would say that.'

Dispassionately, as if he were a stranger on whom I had decided to show pity, I set about doing everything I could to make the rest of my father's life as untroubled as possible. Caring for him meant no more or less to me than caring for the old men and women in the geriatric ward where I had worked as a teenager. I did it out of sympathy for his predicament and out of duty but without much love. I did it because I was still striving to win his approval, to be the perfect son. I did it because it was the easy thing to do. The practical aspects were not particularly taxing, although managing the politics of his sickbed had its complications. Juggling my father's vacillating desires with the demands of his many friends – especially some of his women friends – involved considerable tact.

At first he seemed resigned to his impending fate, which made me proud of him. He was wistful and apparently without regret. 'There is no point in fussing. That's that. *C'est la vie.*'

He slept rather more than usual, developed a passion for drafting and redrafting his will, but otherwise acted as if there was nothing wrong – busying himself with his memoirs, correspondence and visitors. However, his health declined faster than anyone had expected (or I had dared hope) and within a few days of getting home twenty-four-hour care became imperative. As he began to lose strength, so his courage and his temper failed him. He argued with his doctor, complained about his nurses and fretted over his medication. He ranted about Will, who had not yet made it out from England, and

– when he thought she was out of earshot – his main mistress. He had a remarkably low pain threshold (perhaps not that surprising when you consider that he had never really encountered pain in his entire life) and was intolerant of the slightest discomfort. Each day brought a new medical crisis. I was there one evening when he thought he was suffocating and I spent hours on the telephone arranging for oxygen. The next morning his respiratory problems were forgotten and he became close to hysterical that a blood clot was about to explode in his heart.

The fact is, the poor man was terrified.

It frightened me to discover that he was scared. When my time came would I be as ill-prepared? As unable to derive any humour from the situation? It angered me, too. Surely now that he was dying he could set a better example by showing a modicum of acceptance and resolution. Was it unreasonable even to hope that he might at last demonstrate stronger feelings towards my brother and me; say he was satisfied with us; display some sense of responsibility for the unhappiness we had both experienced? His complete lack of gratitude also distressed me. To have enjoyed a long, healthy life wanting for nothing – lovers, family, children, friends, absorbing work, money – and not be thankful struck me as pitiful.

He lay in bed, propped up on pillows, drifting in and out of consciousness, alternately afraid and irate. Will arrived. We took turns to sit with him. For want of something to do, I read my father Wodehouse. Will read him Trollope. In his delirium our father muttered: 'I am right, I know I am right'; 'The end . . . the end . . . the end . . . the end'; 'I was hoping for a better death than this.' And finally: 'Please hold my hand, would you?'

On Monday, 29 March 1999, less than three weeks after falling ill, he died. He was buried, with an irony that would have been lost on him, on All Fools Day. After the funeral Will and I stayed up late clearing out his house. It took us six hours to disassemble his entire life.

I did not cry at the funeral, but later that night, when my own children were asleep, I did weep. I wept for myself, not because I had lost my father, but because I felt alone. I wept because (and this struck me as infinitely sadder) I could not find it in my heart to mourn his passing.

Everyone said, 'How tragic, how terrible for you'. All my life I made an immense effort to be a good son to him. I visited him regularly. I tried to be kind to him. At the end I cared for him – helped him urinate and cleaned his soiled bedpan and mopped his brow with a flannel – though I found it distasteful. I never reproached him. I never burdened him with the troubles of my life or demanded anything of him. Accordingly, his death came as a release.

Now that both my parents are dead I've stopped hating them, started to see the good in them. I believe that before too long I may even begin to love them. Which leads me to wonder whether I will need to die before my own children can be free. Will their happiness ultimately be dependent on my death? If it were so, I would gladly sacrifice my life this very moment.